Naked in the Public Eye

Naked in the Public Eye

Leading and Learning in an Era of Accountability

L. Oliver Robinson

THE SCHOOL SUPERINTENDENTS ASSOCIATION

ROWMAN & LITTLEFIELD
Lanham • Boulder • New York • London

Published in cooperation with the American Association of School Administrators
Published by Rowman & Littlefield
A wholly owned subsidiary of The Rowman & Littlefield Publishing Group, Inc.
4501 Forbes Boulevard, Suite 200, Lanham, Maryland 20706
www.rowman.com

Unit A, Whitacre Mews, 26-34 Stannary Street, London SE11 4AB

British Library Cataloguing in Publication Information Available

Library of Congress Cataloging-in-Publication Data

Robinson, L. Oliver, 1969- author.
Title: Naked in the public eye : leading and learning in an era of accountability / L. Oliver Robinson.
Description: Lanham, Maryland : Rowman & Littlefield Publishers, Inc., 2017. | Includes bibliographical references.
Identifiers: LCCN 2016047567 (print) | LCCN 2016057589 (ebook) | ISBN 9781475832631 (cloth : alk. paper) | ISBN 9781475832648 (pbk. : alk. paper) | ISBN 9781475832655 (electronic)
Subjects: LCSH: Educational leadership--United States. | Educational accountability--United States.
Classification: LCC LB2805 .R685 2017 (print) | LCC LB2805 (ebook) | DDC 371.2--dc23

Printed in the United States of America

This book is dedicated to loving parents who instilled in me the power of perseverance, a loving family who serve as the rock of stability, close friends who foster a deep sense of self, and tremendous colleagues and thought partners.

Contents

Preface

Leadership is disarming and disrobing, akin to being naked in the public eye.

Education leadership is a public act; while results are vital to organizational success they are often scrutinized openly in the name of accountability. People profess a complete knowledge of a leader based only on a tidbit of information, or scrutinize every action based on presumptions, as personified by the African proverb that says, "when the watering hole starts to dry up, even the animals start to look at each other precariously." As a leader, you often feel naked in the public eye.

Leaders who have had truly remarkable careers know firsthand that leadership is paved with a lot of grit, an abundance of hope, and the sheer determination to dream big dreams and strive for extraordinary success. Being a leader for learning symbolizes the power of persistence, the power of perseverance, the power of pursuing a good education, and the power of the dream.

Doors to opportunities are often a result of interactions and experiences beyond one's own doing, validating the premise that to whom much is given, much is required. Life's success is a testimony to the transcending and transforming impact of education.

Naked in the Public Eye serves as a fortification of the commitment of all the true advocates for children, endeavoring to invest in and support children's futures. The content stems from the perspective of a husband, a father, an educator, a witness, and a testimony. It is an articulation of inspiration stemming from a profound excursion of thought and consciousness. Leadership, like life, requires movement from mimicking to manifesting, from imitating to embodying, and always endeavoring to broaden minds and expand cognitive horizons.

The title itself punctuates the tremendous burden leaders carry just by the very nature of being the title holder. Considering all the factors and barriers that leaders must navigate to ensure a safe passage, it is vital that an ample supply of motivation and contextualization of the significance of leadership are provided to fuel the flame of progress.

The book endeavors to spark and support integrative leadership, emboldening leaders for learning. There is a paucity of books and literature about the noncognitive factors such as strategies, attitudes, and behaviors that are crucial to highly effective leadership, hence the compelling need for this book.

Naked in the Public Eye weaves experiential testimony, providing a practical road map to success and illuminating the requisite mental and emotional fortitude. The tone and format are framed to contextualize the complex challenges faced by educational leaders in an era of heightened, incensed-like focus on accountability. The book carefully blends tactical frameworks with strategic soft skills in the sincere pursuit of excellence.

How best to know about the characteristics of high-level leadership than to be able to view it through the eyes of successful leaders? So many people are leading without appropriate support or even awareness of the significance of metacognitive strengths and keen fortitude.

Naked in the Public Eye zeroes in on the pivotal skill set and mentality needed to develop and implement a profound vision for education and foster collaborations that yield life-changing positive outcomes for students.

While processes and best practices are essential ingredients to leadership effectiveness, the sustainability thereof, and the ability to institutionalize positive change result from the empowerment of others, the embodiment of the core mission. *Naked in the Public Eye* takes the reader into the mind of a perspicacious practitioner, providing the opportunity for the seamless embodiment of effective leadership and ultimately the fostering of a "followship" for sustained organizational effectiveness.

The quintessential debate of nature versus nurture—the question of whether leaders are born or made from experiences—still reigns and is exacerbated by the heightened level of scrutiny in an era of accountability. In recent years, the dearth of individuals desirous of entering executive-level leadership in education, namely the superintendency, isn't necessarily a reflection of a shallow pool of certified individuals, but an illustration of the hesitancy to enter the field.

Resultant is the need to provide quality exposure to and insights about the intuitive aspects of the position and the intrinsic rewards garnered from being a leader for learning. It is vital that literature is made available to enhance the knowledge of leaders to be more intellectual, politically sagacious, and intentional.

Naked in the Public Eye serves to open the cerebral pallets, making the prospect of system leadership an attractive option, fortifying the efforts of those on the education battlefield, while sustaining a semblance of sanity in leading the charge to eliminate academic gaps and create opportunity. It is through inspirational leadership that one remains relevant and transformational, forever prepared and willing to audaciously act. If the works are not remembered, they are not maintained. Memorialization is achieved only through compassionate, sincere leadership driven by actions taken from the perspective of forging profound legacy.

Transformational leadership calls for being tenacious in pursuits, garnering support through a keen demonstration of understanding the larger context. It is about having a sincere appreciation of the importance of being able to engage noncognitive, as well as requisite, technical skills. In the darkest hour of need when hope wanes and viable solutions are faint, the execution of the combination of leadership skills transforms the ordinary into extraordinary, and the mundane act becomes transcending.

Naked in the Public Eye endeavors to not only address those traditional tactical skills routinely addressed in leadership texts or readings; it extends to the heart of leadership. It serves to contextualize leadership from a metacognitive and motivational context—the psycho/emotional aspect of leading in an era of accountability—a time when there is a dearth of willing participants, much less highly skilled ones.

There are countless research and books that provide the cookbook approach, but little that speaks to the behaviors, mindset, and mental fortitude required to be effective leaders. The research about intrinsic motivation is interestingly compelling. Recently popularized by the work of Angela Duckworth and *Grit*, the significance of metacognitive motivation on effective leadership has come to the forefront.

Support and practical advice for leaders is provided within an inspirational context. The intent is to summon the grit, the sense of determination to persevere and succeed in the face of tremendous challenge and adversity. Leadership is personal, and while it can be measured by productivity quotients, the sustainability of it stems from conscious efficacy. The book is not a prescription; it is a coupling of intellectual and emotional qualities. The entrepreneurial and fluid nature of leadership is accentuated, as the art and the science of leadership are masterfully illustrated.

The existence and importance of noncognitive skills are contextualized, serving as a supply of knowledge for both sitting and aspiring educational (system) leaders to deal with the quagmires of leadership. The insights shared demystify the personal/professional duplicity and complexity of leadership. *Naked in the Public Eye* is a book for leaders, supporting the often silent side of a very public position.

Chapter One

Moments of Reckoning

> The persistence for equity and the pursuit of excellence are the core stimulants
> of education systems . . . the constructs are not mutually exclusive.

As an education leader, it is clear and evident that the greatest opportunity children can be provided is the chance to get a quality education. Children will, like it or not, fill the voids of their curiosities with information. So, not only is it important what information they encounter but also the source of the information. In other words, a quality education enables children to sift and weigh evidence, discern the true from the false, the real from the unreal, and the facts from fiction.

As an immigrant child to the United States, the charge was simple: take advantage of everything the country has to offer, of which the most important was education. While formal schooling was not my inheritance, wisdom was evident in my rearing. The value of a good education was innately instilled.

The voyage of success is contingent upon knowing that failing does not make a person a failure. Such a philosophy was instilled through both words and deeds, often culminating with pronouncements such as, "Knocked down nine times, get back up ten." It was understood and appreciated that to fail does not make one a failure and the only thing worse than failing is not trying at all.

Complimentary words of wisdom, such as "silver and gold may vanish away, but a good education will never decay" were commonplace in the household. The grave reality that he who controls the diameter of your knowledge also prescribes the circumference of your activities was deliberately instilled in the heart and mind.

1

CRUCIAL CROSSROADS

To punctuate the point, a "moment of reckoning" that transpired in August 1977 at the Miami International Airport is most apropos. Imagine a small boy, just barely eight, who had not seen his father in over three years. The boy and three of seven siblings were filled with excitement to come to America, but more importantly, to see their father, lovingly referred to as "Pops."

From a distance a glimpse was caught causing an impulsive burst, giddily running in anticipation of that big embrace that had been lacking and wanting for three long years. Instead, pure ecstasy and anticipation encountered the astonishment of a profound, lifelong lesson. An abrupt stop in the boy's tracks by a single finger pointed out and a stoic look. What came next were the words that changed the path of history yet written, "You are in this country for one reason and one reason only, and that is to take advantage of everything this country has to offer."

Unraveling from such a ubiquitous web of emotions and the sheer and utter respect for "Pops," an enormous excitement of writing a new chapter of one's life's story was ushered in with unwavering grace, indeed a moment of reckoning. It was the reconciliation of the correlation of hard work to reward. As an eight-year-old migrating to the United States, the land of opportunity, land of milk and honey, and filled with tremendous excitement and optimism, enrolling in school was the ultimate gift.

It is with such internal strength that one counters even the most daunting of tasks and disappointing situations. For it was only shortly after the aforementioned moment of reckoning that another such potentially life-altering experience was encountered. The excitement of learning new things was replaced with confusion after being assigned to a portable classroom, located "over there" far from the main school building, and enduring a teacher who spoke a foreign language for six hours a day.

Befuddled and to the chagrin, apparently, of some wise and learned administrator, who had determined that immigrants from Jamaica did not speak English and hence an ESL placement with Spanish and Haitian Creole speakers was deemed most appropriate. Reflecting back, they were accidentally ahead of the times with multilingual classrooms.

Days of bewilderment lingered in a trailer, a poor substitute for a classroom, with two small, square windows at the top, allowing only the slightest ray of sunshine. To be safe from the abyss of a placement that achieved no more than turning off a young mind from school came at the hands of a lady of tremendous physical stature (as seen through the mind's eye of an eight-year-old) who grabbed one ear and said, "You look like the age of someone that should be in my class, come with me." Perceived cruelty quickly converted into compassion and caring; needless to say, third grade was a delight from thereon.

PASSPORT TO THE FUTURE

As the youngest of eight siblings, seeing the recurring materialization of what was once only a fleeting parental fantasy, each brother and sister matriculated in college. It was exemplified that education is indeed the passport to the future! The more educated, the further the possibility and likelihood of upward economic mobility.

The intrinsic motivation to thrive was eminent; the innate fear of not being good enough or as good. The proverbial syndrome of walking in the shadows of others was pronounced. The skies were made clear, shadows removed, when the ninth-grade English teacher, who was also slated to be the teacher in tenth and eleventh grade as a function of the honors program, said these most profound words, "You are the smartest of all the Robinsons."

It is now evident that at the time it was a mere fib done to boost confidence, but it was a pivotal moment for the inculcation of a sense of significance as a learner. The endorsement of one's capacity to achieve, particularly from someone highly respected, a teacher, musters up inconceivable confidence, boosting academic performance to astronomical heights.

PAY IT FORWARD

There is a responsibility to pay it forward by helping others along the way. Imagine precariously teetering on the pinnacle of future success or misadventure while reeling from the death of a beloved father, mentor, and role model. Imagine being conflicted by the sting of death that leaves an impure emptiness and the instilled lessons of pride and conviction. A week or so later, while walking home from football practice, crossing the footbridge that traversed a canal, the young man, with flashbacks of the emotionally vulnerable eight-year-old, confronted life's proverbial crossroads.

A right turn meant heading straight home. A left turn meant heading toward 5th Street—the gateway to drugs, bars, and gang bangers, all the vices under the sun. A compelling moment of deep contemplation, engulfed with memories of a deceased father and all his teachings and lessons. Piercing words overflowing: "Son, preparation is the mother of luck." "Ambition is the gas of life, step on it, but don't forget the brake of self-control." "Every man has to stand accountable for his actions."

At that critical challenging juncture, perplexed and conflicted, compelled the need to draw impetus from internal strength modeled in unabashed ambition and pride to live up to expectations. Even so, it was evident that guidance from a sage mentor was needed and could only be found by turning left toward 5th Street, toward the path that many young people have succumbed to embrace, a path of potential despair and inevitable disappointment.

On that road to the left was the house of the varsity football coach. Without hesitation the words flowed, "Coach, I want you to be my dad." The response uttered back was not as expected. "Son, I don't have any money to give you, plus, I have two little boys of my own to take care of." Without hesitation, the rebuttal of, "No coach, I don't need your money. I need your guidance," changed the direction of future pursuits.

With coach's help, several full scholarships to prestigious colleges and universities were secured, and ultimately matriculation at Brown University. For the first time, intellectual capacity and academic aptitude were being accentuated as the key to continued success. Brown provided the vehicle to truly "make it" out of poverty and limited economic options; the experience transformed a smart kid into a confident man.

Attending and graduating from Brown University, and later receiving master's and doctorate degrees from the University at Albany, illustrate the transforming and transcending influence of education for me. The moral of the story is that while at times things may appear to be heading down the wrong path, mindfulness is critical. Even along such roads, marked with challenges and pitfalls, opportunities and advantages are apparent when viewed with eyes that stayed on the prize.

Therein rests the will of my ways, the philosophical construct of leadership, and the unwavering and steadfast commitment to quality learning experiences for all students. The prospect of achieving is often predicated on the generosity of individuals and organizations committed to supporting the scholarly pursuits of students, believing in their ability to achieve.

Consequently, there is a profound grounding in the dictate "to whom much is given, much is required." Individually and collectively people have drunk from wells they did not dig and have been warmed by fires they did not build.

Chapter Two

Painting the Picture

> Schools are indeed in so many ways like theaters, the arena where the central dramas of society are played out.

Public education is under fire and increasingly so, with increased accountability juxtaposed against competing interests for scarce means. The reality is that the world of education, particularly public education, is in the midst of a puzzling uncertainty. There is a dire need for keen introspection—meaning undergoing serious soul searching and regaining clarity about what is important.

Inevitably, it is about understanding the need for improvement, what needs to be done and how to best do it. Introspection calls for an individual and a collective recognition that any modicum of success hinges on the favoring of moral conscience over materialistic gains and political expediency.

Being a bystander is not an option, possessing empty hopefulness that others will do it for children—hence, choosing not to become involved but wanting to reap the fruits. The heightened competition for revenue/fiscal support juxtaposed against the sensational push for accountability have spurred on an unprecedented expectation for performance. "Do more with less" is no longer just a mantra, it is a directive. The dynamics of interest and influences has necessitated a commitment to maximize the use of existing resources—leverage opportunities, repurpose when feasible, and restructure or eliminate areas that would otherwise prove futile.

Chapter 2

INEVITABILITY OF THE PACE OF CHANGE

Eventually and inevitably, changing and evolving with the times, maximizing the plethora of scholarly research about how children learn best, and enhancing pedagogy becomes the logical progression in realizing academic success. School systems and education leaders are faced with the awesome responsibility of preparing students in kindergarten for jobs yet to be conceived.

The inevitability of the pace of change has exponentially expanded, creating new challenges for educational systems and the need to be more competitive and increasingly innovative. Being cognizant and careful of the trappings of a consumer society that always teaches and glamorizes the "lack of" is a key step. More and more, people are succumbing to the psychological pull and mental taunting of yielding to the temptations of living up to artificial standards of success, or even beauty.

Without due diligence and caution, a person becomes enamored and engulfed in self-definition based on a façade versus defining one's self based on an appraisal of strengths and weaknesses and the appreciation of each. It is about sustaining a progressive outlook versus gratification that is temporary and fleeting at best.

The articulation of a comprehensive and strategic vision of change and progress is an absolute necessity. A simple, linear, cause-effect approach may miss the fact that today's effect may in turn be tomorrow's cause. A more ecological approach versus a logical approach is at times warranted, having a greater understanding and appreciation of the WHY, the WHAT, and the HOW.

There are a number of ingredients that ensure organizational viability and sustainable progress:

- A clear and comprehensive vision
- A true sense of direction and singularity of focus
- A clear identification of expectations of performance
- Targeted professional development opportunities to hone skills and fine-tune methodologies to provide instruction
- A comprehensive system of support that fosters uniformity and standardization of protocols, procedures, and programs
- An allowance and flexibility for risk taking and creativity

The work of leaders for learning is most essential to the progress of schools, the preservation of a knowledge economy, the fostering and sustaining of an equitable society, and the route and vehicle for upward mobility. Hence, the primary focus of actions and efforts must be on synergism—

maximizing the collective effort, and working in concert and not in competition or contradiction.

In an era of accountability, the terms of engagement have been heightened and the paradigm of success and failure has been warped into a tailspin of uncertainty. The objective of education has morphed beyond simple functional literacy and numeracy into the profound charge of preparing students not only to compete and realize individual dreams, but equally so, to be captains of the global marketplace.

The emergence of technological, economic, political, and cultural exchanges requires a steadfast focus on the advancement of education for all students, not just the elite 5 to 10 percent. Subsequently, the quality of education systems stands as a proven avenue for societal progress and upward mobility.

In many ways it is the definer and preserver of society's moral compass. It is not whether or not schools will change curricula and instructional focus to meet the demand for more technically skilled workers, it is instead a question of how long will it take, and at what cost?

EDUCATION IS AN AXIOMATIC GOOD

The axiomatic nature of education serves to prove all those wrong who are trying to solve tomorrow's problems with yesterday's solutions. Students face the difficult and often unsurmountable task of challenging new norms of excellence. Students are compelled to be smarter and more innovative. Therefore, public schools must be the model of excellence—tried and true.

The goal of education leaders is not so much about only doing the right thing; it is even more so about doing the right thing for the right reason. Consider the common manifestation in the political arena where intelligence and justifiable actions are co-opted by bad intentions and politically expedient compromise.

A quality education serves as the impetus to avoid yielding to the temptation of quick fixes and superficial materialism by equipping students with the internal drive to stop placing more interest in objects and having things and instead embrace moral values and character. The educational pursuit not only yields measurable achievements; it provides enriched opportunities and expanded horizons. Through education students discover and appreciate that it is indeed incumbent upon them to take charge and discover that they can do all those things that they are afraid they can't do.

Consequently, the messaging must be clear and consistent, reinforcing that a student's successful completion of high school is a big deal because it validates the capacity to learn and process complex material and formulate cohesive solutions. It is a big deal because it signifies their ability to endure and persist in the face of adversity for thirteen years. It is, in essence, the lifting of the veil of ignorance, certifying that as graduates they are rational, logical, and learned individuals.

The axiomatic good of education affords students to be liberated innovators, playing in fields that are completely outside the box and ushering in and flowering unimagined creativity and applying the genius of their ideals. A student's high school diploma should unequivocally pronounce that they are indeed ready to be contributing members of an increasingly eclectic society.

EDUCATION IS TRANSCENDING AND TRANSFORMING

The provision of education is complex and challenging, confounded by competing interests. The rewards are undeniably valuable. To that end, the goal of high achievement for all students must stand at the philosophical center of leadership and serve as the catalyst for decisions and actions. An informed and principled strategy must be employed to ensure the vitality of a quality education for all children, regardless of race, creed, religion, or ability level.

The provision of educational excellence cannot be static. Quality is the result of the actions by many. It is about schools and systems effectively meeting their obligations, meaning all students perform at their peak potential. School systems cannot be stymied and dismayed by the challenges of failed reforms and regulatory debacles.

What is the real focus of K–12 systems? Is it to be focused and concerned about graduation under the increased standards? Or, is it to be keenly aware of the need to provide students who will not matriculate in college with legitimate vocational and technical skills to be viable in the workplace? The answer is both, and the same. A graduating class should reflect the multiplicity of success that stems from the multifaceted nature of schooling.

The notion of public schools as being transcending and transforming is being lost in the political melee about school quality, the quagmire of test scores, and the creation of test-taking soldiers. Children and their futures are being used as pawns in a vicious chess game that subscribes to and casts the presumption that excellence is definitive and that success is a preordained prescription.

Not only have educators been left to feel marginalized, students are also being marginalized by the test scores, which in many instances follow racial/ethnic, socioeconomic, and special education demarcations. Students in suburban schools and communities have done significantly better on standardized tests, largely due to those districts having increased parental and community capacity to help support students. The culture of learning and the expectations for performance are exponentially greater, and some of it stems from the simple issue of learning confidence. The student has high expectations of learning, and the teacher(s) has high expectations of learning for the student.

As a result, paranoia of not being adequately prepared to realize success exists among students graduating from high school as they face a world in which education is increasingly essential and knowledge is constantly changing. Fear of inadequacy lives too among parents and is often the flashpoint for politicians and pundits who are fixated on and lament the perceived shortcoming of schools.

The objective of transforming challenges into opportunities and being better because of the experience must be thrust into the prominence of the individual and collective conscience of stakeholders. As a point of illustration, I make personal reference to one of many community service contributions.

As a speaker for GED graduation ceremonies for inmates who took advantage of doing time by constructively engaging educational opportunities afforded to them, this provided firsthand testimony of the transforming and transcending power of education. Recognizing the injustice often doled out by a justice system that has long forgotten the goal of rehabilitation versus punishment, and serving as a role model and teacher of those cast aside as the social underclass—the incarcerated—was not only personally fulfilling, it served a societal good.

Although the stories of those young men's lives had blemished pages marked with pain, regrets, and disappointments, the prospect of educating their minds helped to keep hold of hope, knowing that the story doesn't have to end the way it began or has gone so far. As successful graduates of the GED program, those inmates were saying to themselves and to society that they can and they will do something constructive with the time and the circumstances of imprisonment.

Instead of just serving time of imprisonment, the provision of educational services allowed for the equipping of skills and the garnering of credentials, eventually yielding a contributing citizen upon release—a real step to curb recidivism. Witnessing inmates take advantage of education provisions stimulated contemplation about "What is it that separates me from them, trapped in a world of perpetual doubt, disdain, and despair?" The transforming and transcending power of education serves to recalibrate the measures for success.

It is incumbent and absolutely critical that education leaders remain reverent in reflection. Taking the time to contemplate the work in the appropriate context, lending to the recognition and acknowledgment that when students, incarcerated or sitting in the seats of K–12 systems, dreams are bigger than fears, success is inevitable.

The most significant determinant of success is the willingness to fail in the pursuit of achievement beyond current horizons. It is common knowledge that some of the greatest lessons are realized from experiencing failure. Without the willingness to take risks, trying and trying again, things once deemed impossible would not now be the most notable and useful inventions in the world. Leaders and students alike must have a passion for what is possible.

Leadership must be about action, and leaders cannot be paralyzed by the prospect failure. Leadership, like learning, requires stretching beyond current cognitive boundaries, beyond the known and the natural. It is about embracing the challenges, knowing that every attempt brings great wisdom, hence growing through misadventures versus simply going through them.

Leaders thrive and pursue excellence with almost reckless regard to the unknown challenges. It all starts with the cerebral girding up with the armor of courage and the sharp sword of conviction. It is about fostering and permitting less fear and more resolute action, leading to bold change. If the goal is to get to reward, success is the only option.

There must be a clear recognition, internalization, that in order to do something that has never been done a transformation of perspective and preparation must transpire. There must be a willingness to do the things today that others won't do in order to have the things tomorrow that others won't have. Leading meaningful change in education takes an unwavering commitment to excellence and political savvy.

PROTECTING THE PROMISE

It is said that education is the great equalizer, allowing students to transcend current existence, expand cognitive horizons, and provide limitless opportunities for success. For generations, public schools have stood as the beacon of hope and hopefulness, the gateway to options and opportunities. That is the promise of public education that must be protected by education leaders for all children.

There are very few institutions that have stood the test of time and the voracity of politics. Public education represents seas of possibilities versus silos of predictability. The maximization of opportunities hinges on some key fundamental beliefs:

- Public education is a metamorphic experience for students.
- Meaningful engagement of communities is critical to the success of all students.
- Collaborative relationships benefit the work, which ensures positive student outcomes.
- Balanced assessment approaches including authentic real-world performance benefit students.

- Students need to experience a personal connection to learning.
- An innate desire to learn must be fostered through access to rigorous and relevant learning experiences.
- Intellectual curiosity is neither a luxury nor a diversion; it is the competitive edge.

Protecting the promise means being ardently focused on removing the contradiction of where students are now from the maximization of talents and abilities.

The epitome of hypocrisy as marked by the political acceptance of incompetent performance in the face of ability cannot be accepted. Effective leadership and quality outcomes serve to counteract the rhetoric and bureaucratic accountability efforts aimed at embarrassing and not supporting quality public schools.

A common objective drives the work of system leaders, recognizing that perspectives, opinions, and even expertise change and evolve. The promise of children is always what matters, the bottom line. Education is rightfully about the skills taught, but not to the detriment of the spirits nurtured. Education is a precious commodity.

BEYOND SENSATIONALISM AND RATIONALIZATION

The rhetoric about public schools and education has been sensationalized beyond rationalization. The common mischaracterization of dedicated educators has masked the provision of opportunities for unlimited success for the millions of students passing through the doors of K–12 schools and on to higher education to pursue a productive life.

Contrary to popularized sentiments, public schools serve to ensure that all students develop and demonstrate the knowledge, skills, abilities, and character needed to live useful, productive, and rewarding lives. The objective is to have every student experience a personal connection to learning that will serve them for a lifetime.

School systems, small and large, urban or rural, are committed to providing educational experiences and services aimed at maximizing student potential and aptitude. In so doing, partnerships with families and communities serve to ensure that students will become responsible and well-rounded adults.

Effective leadership dictates an unwavering commitment to academic excellence and to supporting achievement not only in the classroom but also in the arts, athletics, and academic clubs, so all students, regardless of ability or interest, can experience success. What's being tested, while important, is not always the most important.

Chapter Three

Sense of Significance

The end result is having all students fully maximize every opportunity provided.

The challenges faced by society and manifested in schools serve as a vivid reminder that a nation is great not because its economy is flourishing or its army invincible, but because its ideals are indeed loftier. Those ideals must be vaunted in the vision of school systems and paired with the potent leadership to contend with a world that is belied in its incendiary potential.

While the tendency is to languish in and pay too much attention to the prevailing negativity, no longer can despair about the present or anxiousness about the future persist. Subsequently, the fight must be in the best interests of students and efforts must be in concert and not in conflict or contradiction.

Individuals and organizations are called to the forefront, those willing to invest in and support children's futures. It calls for individuals who are truly resolute in their conviction to be champions for children. Obtaining a good education, was, is, and will continue to be the great equalizer.

There exists an increasingly desperate need to help children internalize a sense of significance and preserve their futures. Certainly progress has been made on many fronts, but there is still work to be done. Students and educators alike must all dream big dreams and strive for enormous successes.

As the adage states, "Hope springs possibilities; possibilities ignite motivation; motivation breeds perseverance; and perseverance yields success." While students must be taught to accept finite disappointment, it is more important that they never lose infinite hope.

CONTEMPLATIVE JOURNEY

As forward progress is made, the line to the future must be contemplated and followed with a high degree of confidence that it will end in success. As leaders, so much of what is achieved is only appreciated on a surface or superficial level. There is an intrinsic risk of succumbing to the mere platitudes of efforts, instead of on predicting and preparing for the implications and impact on students.

It behooves one to pause so that hearts and minds can reconcile, knowing that loving the work that's accomplished and doing what is most desirable are often at odds. As members of the most august group of child advocates, an unwavering and undaunting commitment to excellence must be the only benchmark for the countless number of students served across the education spectrum.

Along the contemplative journey, strict and achievable measures of accountability for progress must be defined. During periods of swift transition in which new norms in educational excellence are being defined, educational leaders must pause and appreciate the chance to be an educator and what it symbolizes.

When doubts arise and there are questions about the experience and the challenges of leadership, one must harken back on the legacy of public education and the fundamental charge of being an educator. Not even for a moment can negativity be allowed to cause one to lose sight of the reality that leadership is a calling long before it becomes practice.

Upon taking the contemplative journey of leadership in the new millennium, it is vital that the treatise about schools, reform, and intended outcomes is framed in the appropriate context. There must be contemplation and passionate discussion, even debate, about whether the strict accountability demands of high-stakes testing run counter to pedagogically sound objectives such as teaching students to think critically, to ask discerning questions, and to read with comprehension and intelligent reverence.

OPTING INTO LEARNING

Even in the face of the steadfast focus on testing and accountability measures that have dictated that the only things worth doing are those things that are being tested, the reality still exists that schools are about learning. The job of an educator truly does matter, demanding dedication, caring, and commitment to helping each and every student surpass reasonable, yet high, intellectual standards.

Contrary to popular demands and pronounced political shenanigans, the profession of education is not creating test-taking soldiers in the name of accountability, either for system or for teacher performance. The recent "opt-out" from standardized tests movement is an anomaly, incongruent with the historically significant role of schools being moderators of social justice and the engine for upward mobility.

Instead, the end goal of the profession is to best prepare students to contend with the most rigorous content and appropriately align assessments to measure mastery and progress. A former colleague summed it up best: teachers teach students, not subjects. The imagination does not have to be killed to educate the mind, in that in attempting to cover the curriculum the education of the student is obfuscated or forgotten. As such the search for new teachers is about getting the best, the brightest, and the most caring. Teaching is the great antidote for self-pity.

Schools must make the shift from being distracted with the politics of education to a focus on ensuring that students are "opting" into learning. The process of teaching and learning cannot be bogged down by unyielding processes in the name of accountability for performance, yet also knowing that performance without accountability only yields mediocrity.

With increased benchmarks for achievement and the raising of the bar comes the need for leadership that facilitates school cultures fostering high expectations for students, helping them construct the confidence and motivation required to surpass the academic challenges faced.

With the preeminent mantra being college and career readiness, there must be multiple pathways open to high school students, and it is imperative that students make choices that expand, not limit, their options. Each year and every day, students walk through the main entrances of schools with blind faith that educators are prepared to teach them, to coach them, to be concerned for them, to be prepared for applicable benchmarks, to make them better learners.

Actions and efforts must be about hope and hopefulness, inspiring a sense of inquisitiveness in children. It is about helping to bring students to their preferred dreams: college, career, or otherwise. Public education cannot only be about mandates. Public education cannot only be about tests. Similarly, schools cannot be about the creation of penitentiary-like institutions in the name of school safety, recognizing that the health and welfare of students is a top priority.

So while the debate rages on in the media and in the halls of politics about education reform, the core of the focus is on teaching students HOW to be learners and apply what they learn, providing and ensuring a sanctuary for learning.

CHRONOS AND KAIROS

The talent and genius in every child shines a little brighter as a result of experiences in which education is valued and high achievement is cultivated to be attainable. How then can time be used effectively, predicated on the perspective of the concept of time itself . . . fleetingly or fruitfully? The maximization of time has a lot to do with how it is viewed. In other words, what is done with time is as much a direct function of the perspective about time itself. Time is precious, time is never enough, and yet time is everlasting.

The ancient Greeks had two words for time, Chronos (kroʊnɒs) and Kairos (καιρός). Chronos translates to chronology, chronological; the lock-step progression of time itself, minute to minute, day to day, week to week, month to month, and year to year. Kairos, on the other hand, takes the perspective of time to a new level. A Kairos perspective on time looks at it in terms of meaning, the right or opportune moment (the supreme moment).

The Washington Irving short story about Rip Van Winkle best illustrates the distinction. In the story, Rip Van Winkle slept through a revolution. He went up into the mountains with King George III at the helm and awoke to George Washington as the president.

The story of Rip Van Winkle illustrates and exemplifies the simple but profound notion that school systems can serve either as a place where students merely spend (go through) time or a place where they grow through time. To repeat for emphasis: students can go through time, meaning time is exhausted on the mundane and not necessarily growing over time, or honing one's skills and knowledge.

The dichotomous counterpoint is that while Rip slept (Chronos), the American Revolution was afoot and the concurrent experiences George Washington was having translated to a supreme moment in history as a country (Kairos). So, some key leadership questions about how time is used are raised, both individually and collectively as a system. How is time viewed, and more importantly, what is done with it?

As leaders, is time spent creating memories and experiences that last a lifetime? What experiences will students have during the instructional period? Will time be viewed merely chronologically in nature: period to period, day to day, week to week, and semester to semester? Is it only in Chronos mode, where the mere consumption of time is the end goal?

While schedules and mechanisms help manage time, the true maximization of time comes when the environment supports the ability to be reflective, to live in the moment, and cultivate and foster Kairos experiences. Providing supreme moments filled with countless, profound, life-changing experiences should be afforded to students and adults alike.

The analysis of time from a Kairos perspective undoubtedly speaks to having a leadership focus on identifying and leveraging opportunities. It is easy to have disenfranchisement within the typical transactional model. With a focus on transformation, leaders are compelled to be forward thinking, innovative, proactive, and tolerant of change.

These questions and focus on time inevitably lend to a personal surmise about issues like fairness, engagement, and relevance—about how to interact, interface, and effectuate relationships, with colleagues, students, or even personally. Both the will and the skill, rooted in equity and the firm belief that all children are important, is spoken to.

Hence, the focus is on opportunities that lend to legacy changes that stand the test of time. There are some overarching themes that fuel the perspective on time and subsequent actions:

- Student engagement, helping them find their passion for learning
- Students effectively traversing the increasingly rigorous curriculum across the K–12 continuum
- Students' guided independence, helping students to be in charge of their own learning
- Students' global competitiveness, in terms of the thinking, analysis, and level of student achievement

These themes encompass both chronological timeframes yet are sternly focused on fostering and facilitating Kairos moments.

Engaging in interactive practices and a progressive continuum of opportunities afford options for students to grow and thrive as individuals and as learners. Teachers are to be provided with explicit permission to allow students to facilitate and work in productive groups rather than being the "sage on the stage." Students are to be supported in working to model thinking, creating Kairos moments.

The concept of time, in the context of being Chronos or Kairos, begs the question of the experiences rendered in classrooms. There are countless examples of high-quality teaching and learning across districts, maximizing time, and creating indelible moments of learning; for example, a second-grade classroom in which students read two hours a day using iPads, magazines, and leveled reading books, making the joy of reading infectious. Students are thrilled to read on their own during free reading. When one little girl was asked about her book, she said that she couldn't wait to get back to the book to see what was going to happen next—Kairos moments.

Similarly, in a high school math class students used Chromebooks to flip the classroom. The students made great gains as they did the hardest work in class, together, instead of on their own at home—Kairos moments. The experiences for students should not just be a passing of time but a profound experience to be relished, Kairos moments.

Students live and learn in a very dynamic world, one in which information is constantly changing. It is vital not to fall prey to the battle against time, but instead seek to create Kairos experiences. Those are the moments in life when time itself seemingly ceases to exist due to being totally engaged—emotionally, psychologically, and soulfully. Kairos experiences are the moments when the chronology of time is disregarded and have no bounds—no past or next step—just the moment, when only the experience matters.

Is the educational expedition one that is fleeting or one that is fruitful? Are supreme moments being fostered and facilitated? Are students provided with mere transitions of time (Chronos), or with phenomenal accumulations of Kairos moments? Leadership, both in the contemplative and the practical sense, must foster those supreme moments, taking advantage of those good opportunities.

CHANGE THE WORLD

Students' performance at high levels of proficiency is not optional. As such, a personal obligation to be true to the calling of the education professional is essential. The stakes are higher for students and their parents, and the pressures are much greater on educators to ensure that the focus remains on learning gains and the value-added impact of skills and knowledge acquisition, and not succumbing to a focus solely on assessment gains.

Effective leadership is about embracing the challenge and answering the question: Why not change the world for every child? Why not? Effective leadership is not about mere compliance with state or federal standardized assessment benchmarks. In that same vein there needs to be a firm belief that the goal of education is not merely to obtain and accumulate information, but instead to take what is learned and apply it to create new meaning, contributing to the pool of knowledge.

It is essential that students are shown how to put the knowledge into action, making it relevant. Such relevance is demonstrated by the presence of differentiation of instruction, recognizing the varied learning styles of students as a means to providing an equitable experience of holistic education. There must be a steadfast focus on moving beyond conventional indicators of success. Methods, approaches, and embedded structures must be employed so that students learn in a meaningful context, internalizing the skills obtained and demonstrating applications to real-world situations.

Who is more successful, the teacher who helps a student to overcome a difficult home and family life to achieve in spite of it? Or the one who taught the student who had it all from the start and maximized the potential of their lineage? Or maybe it is the teacher who taught the student who exemplified true grit and resisted the temptation of settling for being average and instead rising to the challenge and achieving beyond all expectations.

TO KNOW IS TO SUCCEED

Some years ago, while driving my son home from lacrosse practice, I found myself embodying my father's character. I told my oldest son, "The name you wear on the back of your jersey represents you, and more importantly represents your family, so wear that Robinson name with pride, with honor, and with an unwavering commitment to fulfill the legacy of those who sacrificed so that you can have the opportunity to wear the name."

The personal reference speaks to a larger issue, the issue of the increasing need for positive adult influence and role models for children. There is indeed something to the old saying, "an idle mind is the devil's playground." In student bodies across the globe are a wide variety of future scholars, community servants, artists, athletes, and just simply great people that need to be acknowledged, recognized, and nurtured.

The beauty of it all is that in the idealistic and often naïve mind of a child they think they are at the precipice of their prosperity. The key then is to keep them filled with tremendous enthusiasm and a sense of wonderment. Needing to know is particularly critical because in so many ways, the new millennium shall be defined more so by the degree of botched attempts experienced than by the marvelous successes that will be taken for granted and viewed as the norm.

Students' successes and efforts must be applauded in order to nourish the promise for greatness to be scholars, to be student leaders, role models, and to be committed to service. Those achievements render personal satisfaction and advancement, serving as monuments of students' contribution and legacy.

Chapter Four

Let Schools Be School

Seek to sanction that which is believed to be the inevitable. Children are more than a data point or red check marks.

In recent years public education has become the target for a barrage of incendiary remarks and comments hurled by overzealous politicians, pseudo-reformers, and opportunistic corporations. There isn't a shortage of solutions/remedies being touted for school turnaround and shrinking the achievement gap, as if it was an illness seeking a medical prescription, all overemphasizing testing and teacher accountability based on teaching to the test.

To accentuate the point, a personal reference is warranted. Early one morning, in the midst of my many discussions with my kids to help program them mentally to maximize the educational opportunities they are presented, my daughter, nine years old at the time, uttered a piercing reminder of what public schools are about:

Today we are wearing pajamas as a way to promote students reading at night before going to bed. So all day today we are going to read and do school, and not do all the mandated stuff.

The story is meant to provide the impetus for deep introspection about the current conundrum of events and transitions afoot. What is happening with public education? Is it risking turning children off from learning in the name of accountability and test scores? How do leaders plan forward in the most seamless and effective manner?

Educators working in the trenches every single day, taking children to new heights of knowledge and mastery, are and always have been the true advocates. However, there has been a torrid whirlwind of negative decrees about the state of public education, leaving more questions than answers:

- What happened to the days of public education being championed as the most noble of all institutions?
- What happened to the fundamental belief that public education is transforming and transcending?
- Words like *reform, accountability for performance, competitiveness, rigor, relevance*, and *college and career readiness* . . . what does it all mean for students, for educators, for education leaders?

The role of public schools as bridges and gateways is being minimized and threatened.

For countless generations public education has transformed the lives of first-generation collegegoers and helped remove the handcuffs of poverty. It has provided lower-middle class families with a beaming sense of pride to have their children receive graduate degrees, some even returning to be teachers in the very same system that gave them an opportunity.

Public education has promoted and supported girls and minorities in pursuit of STEM careers. Provided supports to students with significant learning disabilities and made graduation from high school, college enrollment, and graduation a viable option. There seems to be a lack of understanding and appreciation that schools are designed and geared to teach kids how to learn, to persevere in the face of challenges, to build mental and intellectual stamina, to think creatively, to be risk takers. For those reasons and numerous others, clear articulation of the vision of schools being schools, sanctuaries of learning in many dimensions, is vital.

As society teeters on the precipice of further economic uncertainty, it has become readily apparent that an investment in quality education is the only consistent recovery act. That investment in education, however, is more than mere dollars and cents; it is an investment that demands the uncompromising commitment of highly skilled and dedicated educators to a set of goals and objectives that are rigorous, relevant, measurable, viable, and sustainable.

REMOVING THE CONTRADICTIONS

A quality education is the means by which the veil of ignorance is lifted, igniting the light of genius in each child. Access to and mastery of a quality education enables students to sift and weigh evidence, discern true from false, real from unreal, and facts from fiction. Therein lays the significance of education as a vital investment and the backbone of economic stability.

Removing the contradiction of what schools are and what schools ought to be calls for fostering organizational cultures in which people are willing to put professional integrity first. The priority is doing what is right and best for students, and more importantly not tolerating incompetence or shirking of responsibility by others.

Education traditions and practices of the past are increasingly contradicting with the demands of the future, hence beckoning the cultivation of learning communities in which all customers—students, parents, the community at large—value education and move beyond merely achieving the mandates.

Unlike any other time in history, there needs to be a stern appreciation of the significance of the work and an unwavering commitment to do whatever it takes to promote and facilitate quality learning. It is about a steadfast focus on continuous improvement in the face of insurmountable challenges, the continued realization of success at high levels with increased rigor, even with dwindling capacity to expend more.

These pursuits cannot simply be intellectual exercises, or duplicitous displays of political expediency. Although education is in the midst of enormous changes in testing, in curricula, in evaluation, in accountability for performance and community expectations, increased proficiency in all domains of the school system is a given.

Leaders must be cognizant of and sensitive to the social, emotional, and psychological needs of students and to some degree of the educators themselves, knowing the current stresses of the high-stakes testing environment. Further incentives must be provided and permissions granted for schools to expand the fostering of innovative pedagogy and the development and use of practical assessments that are more than the traditional snapshot approach that now guides the process of teaching and student regurgitation. Education needs to be personalized to students' needs and interests.

Learning in an era of accountability and in a continually changing knowledge economy is integral. Academic success is a bridge from poverty to prosperity. Essentially, globalism has and continues to redefine the benchmarks for success. Graduates of public schools are competing against peers from across the globe, many of whom have a built-in economic incentive, which is the default option of sheer poverty. Education is the ultimate way out for every student.

Removal of the contradictions of past practices, past perspectives, and persistently failing policies ushers in the ability for schools to evolve and function differently and do justice for students in the next five, ten, fifteen, or twenty years.

EXCELLENCE, THE EXTRA EFFORT

The altitude of educational systems is inextricably tied to the quality and dedication of all employees. Success is the only option, job number one. Without a vision of excellence, the system fails, and those who rely on leadership perish. Consequently, decisions made must be linked to intentionally building the conditions for continuous improvement in student learning.

Leadership in high definition embarks upon a movement toward an aggressive reform, summoning enhancements of organizational structures, practices, processes, and programs. The millennium demands proficiency in performance by all students, hence there is a demand for proficiency in performance by and from all educators.

As science has proven, water is extremely hot at 211 degrees, however boiling at 212, providing steam that can propel a locomotive. An extra degree of effort is demanded when going from good to excellent. The challenges faced in education are not new or unique, and most importantly, the solutions are not singular. An earnest embrace of a sense of hopefulness persists. Whatever the mandate, it will be coherent, sequential, and essential to the needs of students, particularly with the overwhelming focus on national core curriculum and international benchmarks.

The simple first step is seriously contemplating the question: What type of education shall be afforded students in the coming days, months, weeks, and years? The promise of success for students should emanate from the compulsion to measure and monitor the success of systems directly by the performance and progress of students. Initiatives must be student centered; hence learning is a direct intent.

A high level of engagement by employees in the vision, mission, goals, and objectives of schools and school districts is absolutely imperative. Students can never be made victims of the ineptitude to commit to success or casualties of systems failing to meet their needs.

RECIPROCITY OF SOWING AND REAPING

Each student possesses a certain inimitable style, a way of being and doing that is uniquely theirs. Consequently, leadership must be focused on helping students harness individual geniuses; hone skills to effectively adapt to the precarious transitions undoubtedly encountered in adulthood. The future is no place for timidity or complacency. It is a place for creativity and boldness in action . . . daring to challenge the status quo.

The goal is to engage in thinking about what is occurring right now, knowing in the same way that sowing and reaping is a reciprocal relationship, so is the transcendent impact of leading on learning. Children's futures are contingent upon outcome. Actions should not simply be responses to mandates. There should be a compulsion to perform at the highest levels.

There must be a meeting of the minds in public education, and more importantly a recommitment to educating children versus merely training them to be compliant. It is about educating children to pose probing questions and to be intellectually capacious. The defining reciprocal moment is a student's graduation or departure from high school.

While it is a momentous milestone, a day of exaltation, a day of ascension, graduation is the result of a thirteen-year climb on the proverbial staircase to the gateway of adulthood, encountering numerous options and opportunities. Over those years students experience success, redraw learning limits, and overcome countless struggles and disappointments. A reciprocal relationship, a direct correlation, exists between the dedicated effort to academic success and the realization of accolades for performance, akin to the reciprocity of sowing and reaping harvest. The seed planted shall determine the harvest—graduation—if the crop is yielded from a consistent commitment to excellence.

So, in that very vein, educational institutions must challenge students to strive for extraordinary successes and not to settle for being just average, for to be average is to be as close to failure as it is to success. In the reciprocal cycle of education, like in life, the end becomes the new beginning. Graduation is not a finish line, but instead another leg of the learning relay. A student's intellectual curiosity is the catalyst, the driving force behind continued success. Subsequently, the blueprint for success must be designed with measurable ends in mind.

The overarching objective is to be systemic and systematic in deliberations, and ultimately in execution. Leaders for learning in an era of accountability must focus on systematizing innovation. Leaders must model and facilitate thoughtful deliberations on how to do things differently, seeking to define and redefine enhanced methods, ultimately stretching the organization's mindset.

CATALYST OF PROGRESS

There must be an unwavering commitment to ensuring a quality education for all children, knowing that the nature of knowledge is rapidly changing and that true learning takes place at the edge of understanding. Education stands as the catalyst to progress and change. To that end, teachers must teach to change the world, helping each child find his or her voice. Excitement about learning causes the gaps in vocabulary and other markers of academic disparity to dissipate, helping children write, rewrite, define, and redefine the paragraph of their predicament.

In a practical and simplistic sense, it is about providing students access to the vocabulary to successfully navigate through the complex web of education. Students must live each moment, inhabit their lives. Each day should be lived to the fullest with a charitable heart and kind spirit, knowing that eternity rests in each moment. Once it is gone, it is gone. No matter what life's transitions—some swift, some painfully slow—the future holds endless possibilities.

Schools have the unenviable charge of preparing students to do jobs that in many cases have yet to be conceived. Initiatives must be student centered where learning is a direct, intended outgrowth and not merely happenstance. An intentional focus on innovation promotes the quest for new horizons, lending to deeper success and abandonment of conventional markers. Just from the pure notion of changing jobs and careers, skill sets must be malleable and transferable.

Schools and systems should foster and facilitate the ideal exemplification of the fervent commitment to achieve in spite of life's circumstances. Regardless of the route taken to graduate, it must be acknowledged that a diploma takes a student into a future yet grasped, opening gates of opportunities to pursue audacious dreams.

As students cross the stage at graduation, palms sweating, hearts palpitating, and even knees buckling—those are all feelings stemming from the excitement of realizing a major milestone of success in the receipt of a high school diploma.

At some point in time a rearview-mirror perspective will occur; what shall be concluded: a regret for opportunities lost, or jubilation knowing that bold and dauntless leadership manifested in progress and prosperity for the next generation? Public schools still are the oasis of enablement for a countless number of students. The value of the education profession, of professionalism, is immense and indispensable. Let's get back to having schools be school, demonstrating an irrefutable belief in the ability of all students; sanctioning what is believed should be the inevitable.

Chapter Five

Leading for Learning

The power of our efforts, of our leadership, of our influence, is multigenerational.

Embracing the doctrine of being leaders for learning means that decisions and actions permeate a collective commitment; an unwavering willingness to ensure that all students are prepared to meet or exceed challenging learning standards and maximize their individual academic potential.

The self-imposed admonition must be an unwavering commitment to fulfill the individual quest knowing that the synergy of efforts will, unequivocally and decisively, outlast, overcome, and transform the greatest challenges into the greatest opportunities. It is not so much about the need to change, to advance, as it is about refocusing efforts, the commitment to take action to achieve exponential results, recognizing that schools function in an environment in which what needs to be understood is still being defined and redefined at an unprecedented pace. Consequently, leaders must possess a 20/20 vision for on-demand education.

As leaders for learning, it is vital that the focus is on bringing about an aligned, systemic approach:

- Communicating constantly
- Possessing a shared set of values
- Hiring for attitude; training for aptitude
- Reinforcing the culture by telling the story of the mission and vision
- Fostering emotional buy-in
- Acknowledging that everyone has value and that everyone contributes
- Being visible—present and modeling

The information turnstile complicates matters, mustering the discipline to employ simple ways to deal with complex issues. The effective transfer of data into information provides a better understanding of students' appetites for learning and aptitudes for achievement.

LEADERSHIP MATTERS

Life at its best is the creative synthesis of opposites. In other words, leaders are at their best when being assertive in pursuits yet humble in the afterglow of achievements. In many ways the perspective captures the significance of leaders, doing the best work when faced with challenges, when faced with competing demands; doing so not for the glory but to support the effectiveness of others.

The leadership focus must be about the articulation of a vision centered on a new paradigm for teaching and learning, enticing innovative practices and enhanced pedagogy. Leaders must promote and personify the values of teaching and learning, which serve as the hallmark of the strength of education systems. The perennial focus must be cultivating school environments where students become independent thinkers, places where creativity is unlocked.

A proven and documented track record of leading complex organizations to a higher plateau of performance must be established and consistently demonstrated. Such bold and progressive leadership is exemplified by the enhancement of curricular offerings and pedagogy at all levels to ensure that not only are mandates being mastered but also that opportunities for best practices are being maximized through the integration of technology into the curriculum and general operations.

Caution must be tendered knowing that as a result of unfiltered and limitless access to information, the risk exists to have a generation of students become more and more knowledgeable about less and less, relinquishing the intellectual capacity, parsing knowledge from disparate fields to formulate novel approaches to enhance human existence.

Congruently, performance accountability is about finding the balance when implementing comprehensive evaluation processes that measure growth and mastery without eroding inquiry and the thirst for learning. Hence, the leadership objective is to hire and develop exceptional teachers to cultivate creativity, possessing intellect and bold thinking.

An unwavering commitment to excellence is institutionalized through effective leadership, the systematizing of highly effective programs, and the cultivation of competency in performance. Ultimately, students' opportunities to explore, to innovate, and to problem solve punctuate the premise of the importance of keen leadership.

Leaders for learning are in prime positions to inspire and aid students in transforming dreams and ideals into the new norms and standards of living. The logic is quite simple; it is all about operating at a new level of thinking, a new level of behaving. It isn't about a quick fix, or a façade change, or a sugarcoating of a harsh reality. It is about the recognition that change is the only constant and stands as the major ingredient for true and sustaining progress.

MULTIPLICITY OF PERSPECTIVES

As one ponders leadership and its impact on the many lives influenced, a multiplicity of perspectives must be considered to avoid succumbing to the human propensity to take things for granted, even life and its swift transitions. The concept of multiplicity of perspectives/views refers to microscopic, kaleidoscopic, and telescopic views.

A telescopic leadership view is more cerebral than practical in that it compels contemplation of the strategic purpose of the organization. *Why* does the organization exist? What is the mission? What are the core values? There is recognition that without a discernment of the big picture, one is merely managing and not leading.

A kaleidoscopic leadership view is broader, taking a generative perspective, recognizing the multifaceted nature of organizations. *What* are the emerging challenges on the horizons, and what must institutions do to evolve in meeting those demands? What needs to be done to be multiplicative as an organization?

A microscopic leadership view takes a deliberate, fiduciary focus. A deep and singular perspective is aimed at asking, answering, and initiating steps to address the question: *How* is the organizational trust being kept? How is the defined or core mission of the organization being preserved?

The need for leadership to take a multiplicity of perspectives intimates that while the length of leadership service is ultimately not controllable, its width, depth, and meaning to others is a deliberate choice. A steadfast commitment to excellence, fueled by the need for continued growth as a leader and the multifarious vision inherent in educational systems, is essential.

Engaging a multiplicity of perspectives as a leader is good insurance for continued progress. A myopic perspective lends to the inevitable demise of any program simply because the pace of change is fast and increasingly uncertain. Hence, effective approaches to education are dynamic, fluid, and engender an organic involvement of stakeholders.

The multiple lenses model, by which leadership decisions are viewed, is predicated on the fact that if two people look at the same issue from different vantage points different conclusions will be drawn. Therefore, a multiplicity of perspectives must be employed when leading to foster and facilitate stronger pedagogy and to support instructional leadership. Ultimately, a triangulation of efforts aimed at addressing the variety of needs and demands students encounter yields improvements in performance.

To examine the value of employing a multiplicity of perspectives, an example can help highlight the depth of understanding for problem solving. Take the debate that rages with teacher and principal evaluations, Annual Professional Performance Review (APPR). A telescopic view means taking a strategic perspective, contextualizing the implementation of APPR within the broader organizational objective.

A telescopic view leads to the realization that APPR is a function of the "re-norming" of public education, subsequently provoking key "Why" questions being asked and answered. Why is it important to have a high-quality evaluation model? The "Why" question keeps the focus of teacher evaluation on:

- Ensuring student engagement
- Helping students find their passion
- Providing guided independence, helping students to be in charge of their own learning
- Learning with the long-term view in mind

Similarly, the "Why" questions keep the focus of principal evaluation on:

- Improving student achievement by cultivating and supporting learning through comprehensive, rigorous, and coherent curriculum and high-quality instruction
- Driving change focused on students' global competitiveness—college and career readiness
- Having a continuous growth model to think differently about learning

The telescopic perspective coerces the examination of an issue not only from what matters but also why it matters. The "Why" perspective reveals the critical need to convey a strong and clear message that the synergy of the collective efforts is focused on the common goal of raising students' outcomes.

A kaleidoscopic view takes on a generative perspective, meaning answering the "What" question. It is a multiplicative view, recognizing that there are multiple moving parts. What emerging challenges are schools facing? What new strategies need to be generated in order to meet the multiplicity of challenges? What needs to be done to be deemed effective?

In the case of the APPR process, the vital question becomes: What is the intended outcome or objective of teacher evaluation systems? Correspondingly, the focus is on the teaching and learning process. Systematizing expectations and implementation of innovative practices and inquiry-based pedagogy to respond to student needs and facilitate intellectual engagement are punctuated.

A view of teacher evaluation from the "What" vantage point induces the need to effectively address vertical alignment, structured continuum of spiraling curricula articulations, and pedagogy. The interdisciplinary application of Common Core Learning Standards is placed front and center. Pedagogical alignment with the way students learn is the predominant shift. Parental engagement/understanding of new curricula and assessment become a system norm. The intersecting of personnel, budget constraints, and demand for highly effective staff is an essential objective.

A kaleidoscopic view of APPR accentuates the flexibility and adaptability to ensure that performance management processes are administered with fidelity by taking multiple aspects of the organization into consideration at the same time as decision making. For instance, nondirect instructional supports are aligned with instructional demands. Interventions such as coteaching or specialized instructional programs are illuminated as part of the general education curriculum mapping. Engaging such a view enables higher-level instructional practices to become a reality in classrooms.

The net result of the appreciation of a kaleidoscopic view is the fostering of pride in school and quality in every dimension, engrained in culture and actions. Teacher development shifts the focus to deeper practice and a positive learning experience. The evaluation model is inherently incentivized, better execution translates to better scores for teachers/principals, and subsequently it leads to better student performance. It is the added leverage for sustained growth.

A microscopic view, a fiduciary perspective, focuses on answering the questions of "How?" How is trust kept? How are requirements being fulfilled? How is utterly failing being avoided? How are those things most critical to success being honed in on? As school districts make shifts to new curricula resources in an effort to meet the demands of Common Core, the question arises: How do teachers best implement what is being purchased and effectively evaluated accordingly?

Consequently, implementation of APPR from the microscopic view lends to the effective connection of assessments to learning—moving away from assessments for teacher scores to diagnostic assessments used to enhance or modify instruction. The analysis and synthesizing of evaluation data into information allows for engaging in on-demand professional development and conversations about instruction. Directly related is the need for effective progress monitoring—analysis of data to identify, predict, and forecast performance trends, and teachers demanding data and even challenging administrative use of data—a true data culture.

Subsequently, school principals must now engage in effective instructional leadership with intense accountability for performance. Deliberately and assertively scheduling to maximize availability and contact time with teachers and students becomes the norm. A common language regarding the specific areas of classroom practice is established, setting clear targets for good teaching/good instructional leadership.

A microscopic view yields assurance of inter-rater reliability in completing evaluations. The synchronicity of comprehensive data sets and systems allows principals to identify and dissect performance trends, transforming data into information to make decisions. It transforms the evaluation process from a challenge into opportunities for administrators to immerse themselves in curriculum, progress monitoring, and performance results.

Engaging an assortment of perspectives—telescopic, kaleidoscopic, and microscopic—provides enhanced leadership clarity. The multiple lenses reveal that ultimately leadership is about leveraging the capacity to enhance the experience and achievement of students. In the case of the APPR process, the objectives and the actions required to effectively evaluate quality pedagogy and instructional leadership are clear and evident. Students are assessed only for measuring learning by the administration of relevant, quality assessments. Growth and achievement measures are formulated to reflect trends in student learning. Information is clear and easily understood by students and parents alike, yielding independence in learning and increased parental engagement.

The multiple perspectives approach ultimately ensures a triangulation of involvement—student, parent, and staff—in the learning experience, aiding in navigation of the complexities of education systems that are increasingly inundated with competing interests and a limited capacity to address the diversity of needs. Leadership from a multilenses perspective is fundamental, now and into the future.

ADAPTING TO THE CHALLENGES

The terrain is no longer discrete and concrete but virtual and multifaceted, connoting future progress. Leadership goes beyond mere mastery of "technical skills," recognizing that certified does not necessarily mean qualified and capable. Leadership supersedes traditional management, which seeks to merely preserve past accomplishments.

Leadership matters in resolving adaptive challenges and changing people's values, beliefs, habits, ways of working, or ways of life. It is about mobilizing schools, families, and communities to deal with difficulties. It is about tackling issues that society often prefers to sweep under the proverbial rug.

Consequently, leadership is often personally difficult and professionally dangerous. It is about saying what needs to be heard rather than what is preferred. In the end, leadership is more than the employment of simple, technical solutions. It's about problem resolution and addressing adaptive challenges through the synergistic efforts of personnel, a commitment by all to work in concert and not in contradiction.

Leadership involves challenging people to reconcile the contradiction of espoused values and actual behavior, facing up to frustrating realities. It is not simply about changing the brake pads when frequently worn down by poor driving habits; it's about compelling change in the habit of driving with one's feet on the brakes.

As education demands become increasingly complex, leadership will matter more because it will be less about controlling the environment of schools and more about facilitating engagements. It is about . . .

- Being people experts with a sound understanding of the enterprise
- Being transformed by the renewing of the mind
- Recognizing that not all have the same skills and expertise
- Holding others to work to the proportion of their talent
- Simplifying the complex with diligence and hopefulness
- Being fervent, not slothful
- Being resolute and honest in all pursuits

The paradigm shift in leadership to address adaptive challenges parallels the redefining of the mantra that the true value of education has moved beyond merely teaching content to producing fluid, dynamic, and adaptable learners. Shifting dictates the ability to shuffle and effortlessly take three distinct tactics: inspiring (allowing), embarrassing (encouraging), or mandate (requiring). In essence, quality leadership matters and is about using complex skills to bring about practical solutions.

Chapter Six

Vision–Embodiment–Empowerment

The road to excellence is never ending, often unpaved, uncharted, and traveled with a high degree of trepidation.

Appreciating that quality leadership is a guidepost versus a hitching post, being a student of the profession is essential. Learning to lead is an endless endeavor. It is about ensuring that leaders do not become "phylogenic" in their approach. There must be a willingness to adjust and embrace change and challenges; knowing that contrary to popular demand, being omnipotent is a fallacy. Oftentimes a leader really doesn't know what needs to be known, yet must still take action. To that end, effective leadership must consist of three distinct but intertwined components: *Vision (predict it) > Embodiment (live it) > Empowerment (let others live it).*

Formulating and articulating a vision in the face of competing interests and the increasing demand to sustain the fiscal and physical capacity is of utmost importance. A leader must be clairvoyant, able to discern the big picture, and see the ultimate end goal: the provision of the best options for all students to succeed through technological advancements, academic supports, and diversified teaching/learning styles.

Once articulated, the actualization of the vision is contingent on motivating buy-in. The embodiment of the purpose is a notable outgrowth of quality leadership. Knowing that nothing ventured is nothing gained means inspiring personnel to be magnetized by the motion of progress. Conversely, resting on the laurels of past accomplishments translates into the conservation of inertia and avoidance of muscular approaches to advancement.

Embodiment entails striving to always do what is best for students and not be enticed to cater to the whims of adult conveniences or succumbing to the pitfall of immediate gratification. Embodiment is indeed the possession of a true conviction to the noble profession of education.

Engaging in the deliberate building of the conditions for continuous growth and improvement epitomizes empowerment: letting others live it, not just some and some of the time, but giving permission and allowances to do so all of the time.

Empowerment is a challenging aspect of leadership, pushing for continuous improvement and increased productivity by arousing emotion, provoking thought, and engaging in passionate and unfiltered debate. Seeing it, allowing others to live it, and empowering action is done within an accountability structure, holding self and others responsible for actions and outcomes. At the center is the willingness to ask tough questions and make hard decisions, satisfying mandates with fervor and embracing and engaging the public with fidelity and an unwavering sense of integrity.

PERSONAL INTEGRITY

The professional ethic of any good leader is to provide good and credible service, and ensure others do the same. Subsequently, leaders serve as the catalysts of progress yet to be contemplated. Educators are the keepers of promises yet defined. These revolutionary times of educational renorming are reserved for those who can possess authority with compassion, might with morality, and strength with sight/vision. Simply stated, leaders must be compassionate and caring, not calculating and cunning.

Leadership is personal. It is all consuming and requires sincerity and conviction. The anchor to effective actions is an assured sense of morality and integrity in a world plagued by the sport of hate hurling, cynicism, venomous criticism, blame, and condemnation. Succumbing to the toxic commentary and forsaking the proposition of expert leadership is not an option. Leadership presence and ultimate influence in the life of a child demands determination and diligence in deliberation, decision, and demonstration.

It is beyond a superficial declaration of commitment to excellence for students. Leading with integrity is an enthusiastic embrace of accountability for every action and every interaction. Deeply declaring and firmly demonstrating accountability for the success of all students personify and exemplify performance excellence. The accountability is rendered individually and collectively.

A sense of personal integrity solidifies a true commitment to pragmatically embracing the challenges afoot with a keen sense of inventiveness. In the midst of a muddled and untidy period of reform, stemming from multiple and simultaneous reform initiatives, such conviction to creativity is particularly critical. Leadership thrives through inventiveness, individually and collectively, doing what must be done to ensure education continues to be transforming and transcending for all students.

Personal integrity demands tapping into the expressed passion for teaching. The active modeling of a gold standard of professional ethics undoubtedly yields professionals who embrace the challenge. Growth without being prompted and probed to be better is the true mark of personal integrity. Integrity means consistently endeavoring to maintain untarnished reputations as consummate professionals, always standing firm in the commitment to do what is fair and equitable for all students.

Such a realization is only feasible if educators, as policymakers, as advocates for children, as leaders work in one accord, in concert, and not in contradiction. It is that same passion that must be translated to quality learning and high performance for all students.

The satisfaction of parental expectations that all will be done in the best interest of students is job one, for everyone. Students, staff, and communities depend on leadership to carry the mantle of right and righteousness and the torch of truth and trustworthiness. Educators hold sacred and historically reverent positions—the people who students remember. Consequently, not only is it a legal and professional responsibility to ensure that the best interests of students are taken into consideration, it is an ethical duty to do so.

As leaders for learning, influential members in communities, and the bearers of the moral standard. At the end of the day, it is about personal integrity; committing to continuous improvement to enhance skills so as to yield a better result. For all those reasons and countless others there must be resolute focus on being the thought-leaders in a reform-stricken era. Every day and every experience must be approached as a proving ground for innovative and engaging practices, done with pride and a veracious sense of integrity.

SYNERGY OF EFFORTS

Systems can be no better than the men or women who compose them, relating back to the significance of empowerment. The organizational culture of school systems must be built on functional teamwork, meaning everyone (educators, students, and parents) is present, participating, and fully engaged in the process of deciding and doing, while it can be painfully difficult at times to realize and to maintain. Therefore a dogged determination to avoid succumbing to the comfortable lull of the status quo and complacency is indispensable.

A leadership prerogative therefore has to be organizational responsiveness; contagiously inspiring and motivating staff to be excited about change.

The endeavor to affect change, however, need not always be about creating or defining new landscapes. Oftentimes it is about looking at things through new lenses—lenses of enthusiasm for more purposeful actions.

In so doing, there needs to be an embrace of the unknown future with unabashed excitement, like riding a roller coaster in the dark. Not knowing what is around the next bend or when the next sudden drop will occur yet still screaming at the top of your lungs with excitement and liberating joy.

Promoting synergy in effort is a daunting task indeed, but one that must be encountered and conquered. These are unprecedented times, an era of increasing accountability that requires being ambitiously transformational, realizing synergy takes a mentality, a singular focus on constantly driving to improve, converting followers into leaders and leaders into moral agents.

The adage that the amount of enthusiasm at the beginning of a task is disproportionate to the amount of enthusiasm at the conclusion of a task rings true. Leadership is truly about initiating muscular approaches to advancement, marked by an unrelenting commitment to industrious pursuits and making a positive and lasting contribution.

Leading for learning not only implies the execution of strategic actions; even more importantly it dictates the empowerment of others to lead, regardless of title or position, the synergy of efforts. These types of symbiosis play out in schools when educators embrace students who in turn become independent thinkers, helping to facilitate the ability to be conveners of individual destinies.

The synergistic efforts of committed leaders for learning make the magic of learning come to life. Teachers must all be highly qualified and highly capable, as measured in three primary domains:

C: Content Knowledge—academic rigor and relevance
P: Pedagogy—art and science of teaching
R: Relationship—positive engagements to ignite the passion for learning

Ironically, the characteristic that is least emphasized and yet is the most influential and significant is the ability to establish motivated and productive relationships, the emotional commitment—a sense of caring and compassion.

The current era of accountability demands a willingness to work interdependently toward the common goal of performance excellence, and in turn avoid the blind spot that impedes achievement. An interdependent approach allows for evolutionary change in schools: being much more proactive, seeking out new ideas and ways to measure and communicate results, and recognizing and celebrating performance excellence.

To punctuate the point, think of the analogy of thirty thousand runners in the New York City Marathon: all have a common goal, but they are not a team because they are not working interdependently. True synergy of efforts requires more than a common goal, but rather a unified, convicted goal.

DIFFERENCE MAKERS

Leaders for learning in an era of accountability must hasten to heed the charge to be difference makers by striving to be at the frontier of competence and acknowledging and learning from incompetence. Choosing the calling compels standing up and being champions for every student, every time. There is no place to be faint of heart, or conflicted in philosophy about the impact of education.

A successful school system reveals dedicated, student-focused educators. External forces are used as the impetus to innovate, engage best practices, and be a presence in the daily lives of students. The accountability, the embodiment, and acceptance of the significance of leadership roles and re-sponsibilities are paramount. The heart of accountability is focused on being true and real models of excellence, the embodiment of professionalism.

The authentic desire to succeed as a difference maker, the desire to make a marked contribution, is inwardly motivated, and comes from deep within the soul. That type of intrinsic motivation compels actions that are beyond the sole pursuit of material gains, for such pursuits can leave a feeling of being curiously empty and oddly without meaning. While the job requires a personal commitment, it is not personal in that objectivity rules the day and deliberations.

The professional obligation of educational leaders is the fostering of envi-ronments that are conducive to learning and pedagogical mastery. Conse-quently, leaders for learning in an era of accountability must function from the fundamental perspective that education fosters hope and instills ambi-tious pursuits. The goals are quite simple:

- Keep kids in school and teach them within a network of suitable role models that provide exposure to culture, college, and careers
- Maintain high expectations for performance
- Foster enduring partnerships for attainment and equitable distribution pro-visions
- Parent the parents—stop the intergenerational cycle
- Instill confidence that delay does not mean denial, while building on strengths, not harping on deficits
- Focus on the ingenuity and creativity, and the unprecedented coping skills, inherent in children

Using a personal reference as a point of illustration, serving as an algebra teacher at an alternative school provided the tremendous opportunity to en-gage some of the most imaginative and innovative students. One in particular was a known drug dealer. Each time he was asked to come to the board and do a problem, he refused.

So, instead of engaging the student from a disciplinary perspective, engagement was from a learning perspective, considering the student's lens of the world. The enticing question was one of relevance, questioning the methods of assurance used to avoid being cheated when selling drugs on the streets if the self-proclaimed lack of and interest in learning math were true.

A methodical articulation was engaged of how kilos are translated into ounces, and then formulating a market rate and the designation of a profit margin on each sale. Needless to say, the student knew more about mathematics than most teachers of the subject. With a lot of reassurance and support, a brilliant mind eventually enrolled in college to apply knowledge in a way that avoided penitentiary as the final outcome. Many stories like it play out in the halls of schools across the nation, signifying the value of quality schools.

Think about it: a teacher's accountability hinges on a student's success. A student's success hinges on a teacher's performance, which is impacted by program and curricula design and pedagogical mastery, which speak directly to teacher preparation and the leadership capacity of school districts to provide ongoing professional development and innovativeness.

FUNCTIONAL GOVERNANCE

Contrary to popular demand, educational leadership is not just about curriculum and instruction, nor is it just about dollars and cents. An administrator's accountability, be it department, building, or district level, hinges on effective program design, execution, and provision of support. Effective system leadership ultimately rests with a functioning board governance and administrative synergy. Policies must support the goals and objectives of the school district.

Relatedly, clear and consistent practices and protocols are sustained within the culture of the organization. As leader-servants, helping the school and the community realize the goal of providing a high-quality educational experience, there is a keen acknowledgment that a school system can only go as far as the community is willing to support it. Consequently, it is vital that the interactions and engagement with the board of education and key community stakeholders are singularly focused, creating the conditions for learning. Functional governance is driven by an unwavering focus on the goals of the district.

With almost a decade and half in system leadership, there have been many experiences with new board of education members, some faithful to the district mission, others politically charged by single issues. However, there has been very little turbulence. It is incumbent on a system leader to articulate and reinforce to board of education members that the district is a system made up of many parts, of which the board of education is one key component.

A healthy superintendent/board of education (BOE) relationship is critical for a school district functioning, affording the opportunity for organizational advancement. Effective leadership and governance is about being able to take positive actions, make value-added investments, and leverage opportunities to enhance the district's capacity to provide a quality educational experience for students. Conversely, an unhealthy BOE/superintendent relationship manifests into being trapped in the morass of ineffectiveness and waste.

A healthy relationship sends a resoundingly positive message to the school and the community at large, fostering a sense of confidence and subsequent support from the public, as apparent at school budget votes. The public referendum is more than just dollars and cents; it is a gauge of voter confidence.

Keys to make such a relationship work include:

- Public acknowledgment of service—board of education members supporting the district's commitment to excellence.
- Consistent communications—never have the board hear news from other sources first. Every Friday the board of education gets a correspondence, as simple as a brief email update or an executive summary report on key items or occurrences.
- Provision of a road map—a plan for board of education presentations or information sharing throughout the year on key events and activities that are aligned with the district goals.
- Clearly define roles—leadership versus governance, done through a combination of an extensive orientation for new board of education members and an annual retreat of the board of education.
- Promote professional development opportunities—join board of education members at conferences and workshops.

Some of the pitfalls to effective leadership/governance:

- Forgetting that it is the collective effort that drives change, not the arrogance of any one person
- Not communicating at all or not communicating equally with all members; information sharing levels the playing field
- Getting too close, forgetting the boundaries of the legal and formal role of the board of education members; a healthy formality is important
- Sharing confidential information outside of executive session
- Inconsistency in demeanor and approach.

Disagreements among superintendents and members of the school boards are bound to happen. To avoid confrontations, the following stipulations in the superintendent's contract have proven to be effective:

- No surprise contractual clause—stipulation that any issues or concerns shall be brought to their attention within twenty-four hours avoids a mole hill growing into a mountain
- Clear stipulation about the evaluation process, instrument, and timeline
- Clear understanding that the goals of the district drive the administrative focus, and subsequently, the basis for assessing leadership effectiveness
- Scheduling of regular meetings, at least every other week, with the board of education leadership (president and vice president) to discuss matters and preemptively address problems

Bottom line, regardless of the challenges that lie ahead, intentions and subsequent actions must be strident and intentionally positive. Be clear, honest, and lead with conviction—there may not always be agreement, but respect will not wane.

The tenor of the times dictate that leadership and governance alike must take stock and complete a serious assessment of how business is completed and expertise maximized. Subsequently, school districts' leadership and governance must be committed to providing a continuum of effective strategies, opportunities, programs, and services that embrace learning as the fundamental mission of schools. A comprehensive and synergistic set of goals with a unified focus, consistent processes, and an embracing organizational culture is indispensable.

Chapter Seven

Position for Prosperity

Progress can be messy. The end may not be clear, but forge ahead . . . education is a precious commodity.

Schools serve as the opening of new gates, the gateway to unseen, undefined, and endless possibilities for students, allowing for the ascension to heights of doing and achieving. Learning is a deliberate and time-consuming process. Initiatives must be student centered, hence erasing the dogmatic posture of teaching as primary and learning as a happenstance. The focus must be on ensuring the district expends on initiatives that promote the continued development and implementation of high-quality educational programs that prepare all students for the transition to the more demanding high-tech, globally competitive market.

Contending with public scrutiny is about balance, realizing assessment benchmarks, and ensuring that a true sense of inquiry and love of learning is being inculcated for all students. Subsequently, in the same way that a perspective on faith defines the parameters of one's personal sense of persistence, the belief in the brilliance that rests within every child defines the work of leaders for learning, endeavoring to preserve and enhance the quality of education.

AMBITIOUS SPIRIT

As leaders the goal is to make organizations ambitious, an attitude and organizational culture that consistently and continuously looks at what is possible. Such ambition spurs from being imaginative about what can be done better for students. It is the willingness to expend capacity (programs and processes) and provide the requisite support to make consistent improvement possible. There must be an ardent demand for the degree of rigor and discipline that will ensure the best result, such as having students own their learning.

The self-imposed parameter of being "done" learning is abandoned and substituted with the prominent fostering of a steadfast determination to explore what else is possible. The notion of stopping at the "fix" is replaced with delving into understanding and influencing the root causes of problems, dissecting the layers.

Leaders must master the art of being intentional; paying attention to one's intuition, but questioning it to ensure validity or basis. Once the conclusion of a task is achieved or perfected, it becomes the basis or springboard for the quest to propel to a new plateau of being and doing. Ambitious organizations boldly give permission to risk-taking, organizational cultures that speak to always seeking to improve.

Subsequently, effective leadership is now all about being able to recognize inefficiencies in their infancy and proactively planning and implementing cost-effective measures while maximizing the expertise and competence of employees. Consequently, certain characteristics of highly skilled professionals must be upheld and molded:

- Organized and Focused:

  - Make the experience relevant and related to the experiences and interests of students
  - Fuel a sense of inquiry and desire to learn new and more challenging things

- Communicate by example:

  - The embodiment of being respectful, genuinely compassionate, and optimistic about students' success
  - See the opportunity and don't become dismayed by only seeing the disparity
  - Change the concept of mistake into the construct of new learning

- Wisdom:

  - Capacity to recognize the complexity of functioning without being immobilized by it
  - Find the simplicity on the other side of complexity by questioning conventional thoughts and beliefs
  - Revise and persist as learners

- Enthusiasm:

- Possessing the "whatever-it-takes" attitude
- Imparting nothing less than the very best effort
- Being students' best advocate for their success

Effective leadership dictates involvement with a wide variety of organizations, lending talents to numerous initiatives aimed at improving the quality of education. The model also extends to concerted efforts to foster articulation agreements with higher education institutions (preparation programs), teachers' unions, and state education departments to ensure that degree and graduate programs that certify educators have as the primary goal the provision of highly balanced and effective teachers.

The need to foster an ambitious spirit is exemplified by the dramatic change in the job description of a teacher (especially at the elementary level) over the past years, compelling the development of more rigorous standards for preservice teacher prep programs. Such partnerships demonstrate the need for a P–16 philosophy of education, including the local business community.

Teachers and staff come on board with varied experiences; therefore, orientation is important. In so doing, it must be made clear that employment with the school or district is not a result of compulsion or constraint but a conscious selection of the best. It is a privilege to be a part of the learning community. With that privilege is the responsibility and expectation that each will give his or her all to the betterment of each other and every student.

An ambitious spirit all comes down to a sincere appreciation of the quality that each employee brings to the table. Tapping into the aptitude for inquiry and the disposition to think globally in conjunction with enhancing and expanding the scope of professional development is the X factor. An ambitious spirit allows for contending with the inevitable instability of regulatory changes, fiscal concerns, and continued budget constraints.

The stark reality is that as the stakes for students have been heightened, the availability of funds has tightened. The organizational culture needs to promote an ambitious spirit, reflective in all that is done, from instruction to operations. A shifting of the equation inculcates the assessing schools and systems performance from looking at PAST + PRESENT = FUTURE to the perspective that when performance is discussed it is about the future. The past is prologue; and while the present moment is fleeting, the future is a proliferation of present moments.

MOLD MINDS AND SHAPE FUTURES

Popularized phrases such as "success is often not determined by what happens, but the reaction to what happens" and "not by what life brings, but by the attitude individuals bring to life" punctuate the point of positioning for prosperity. Leadership that is always forward thinking and willing to take the bold steps to continuously improve the quality of education is an imperative.

The organizational tone and tempo must speak to the belief that every child will learn. Being an educator is not just a job—it is a calling. It is a tremendous opportunity to mold and shape a young person into a vibrant, confident, and productive adult. Success of students has to be required. There can be no other option. Now more than ever, education is each child's best hope for a bright future. There must be a willingness to step out on faith knowing that core beliefs are key determiners of success.

At the center of positioning for prosperity is the existence of a passionate belief in a students' capacity to achieve. The provision of education must be from the optimism of the will and not the pessimism of the intellect. Essentially, students must be inspired, motivated, and supported to possess and exude a genuine excitement about learning, dissipating the gaps in vocabulary and other markers of academic disparity.

Prosperity therefore translates to mean that students are sagacious enough to avoid becoming a party to or victim of fact-free pronouncements. Students must indeed be able to walk through life with their eyes wide open. In so doing, there are a few cautions to be considered. It is essential that students are mindful that they live in a time in which unfiltered thoughts are spewed across cyberspace or anonymous sound-offs in local newspapers.

Students must be learned enough to see the piteous shield of indignation and intolerance for what it is, and instead be guided by the simple values of respect and care. The polarization of political perspectives has created a senseless new reality for students. Words and actions are chosen to engender a certain reaction rather than based on genuine and sincere thoughts.

As future leaders, students are the galvanizing forces to ameliorate classism, diminish achievement gaps, and cause social divisiveness to be relics of the past. The type of prosperity needed serves to inspire students to become legends, not in their own minds, but in their time. They can have a transformative impact, striving to possess a larger-than-life quality and knowing that today's impossibilities become tomorrows' norms.

The potential of students is boundless, making the need to position public education systems for prosperity even more critical. Graduation from K–12 public education systems must continue to be a landmark in society, defined as being familiar yet prominent and distinctive.

CONDITIONS FOR LEARNING

The cultures of schools must be defined, fostered, and facilitated by keen leadership. The sole objective should be the building of the conditions for continuous improvement in student learning, which means vibrant partnerships that promote internal and external networks. At the center of it all is the recognition and internalization that school plays the dominant role in exemplary performance, and school leaders play a critical role in shaping the elements of success.

As higher expectations and standards of performance make the mission of the district more demanding, rising costs and taxpayer fatigue make the leadership responsibility more challenging. Ultimately, it is about marshaling every asset of the school district in the service of student achievement, and certainly fiscal leadership sits at the center.

Being good stewards of increasingly scarce resources is a crucial role of leadership. With that comes the necessity to seek out alternative funding sources to support creative and innovative best practices. A goals process, focused on maximizing individual and collective leadership, is requisite.

As such, schools must have strategic goals that align and support the broader vision. From enhanced processes for evaluating teachers and administrators to the institutionalization of the shift to the Common Core curriculum, strategic efforts must ensure the optimal success of all students. With numerous changes afoot, suddenly the world is at the doorsteps of schools.

NOT AN IDLE INTELLECTUAL EXERCISE

Although some systems are doing brilliantly with some students, far too many students are still succumbing to institutional pitfalls as illustrated by the inability to meet the demands of the battery of state and local assessments. It is absolutely critical that schools and systems truly come to grips with the reality that every child that walks through the halls deserves the best possible opportunity for success.

In the midst of accountability crises, leaders must stand tall, serving as the beacon light of hope that brightens the paths of those in despair. Educational leadership, however, goes beyond only engendering and inspiring students to dream and be motivated by the presence of hope; it calls for actively paving the pathways to that realization.

Seeking to control the destinies of schools and systems by keen and scrupulous use, to support and foster creativity in the delivery of curriculum and services, is critical for leaders in an era of accountability. The resonating feeling is being overwhelmed by the numerous tasks at hand, or is distracted by the sentiments of those who are disgruntled by the mere prospect of change and progress. It is not merely an intellectual exercise.

The focus has to be on the allocation of funds to ensure that steps are taken to directly impact the end result: creating and sustaining the conditions for high-caliber learning experiences. Decisions that provide schoolchildren with inadequate facilities and insufficient resources and then brand them with the label of failing must be vehemently protested. Such actions are tantamount to cutting off the legs of a man and then condemning him for being a cripple.

The institutionalization of highly effective models for teaching and learning must be commonplace. The instructional focus must shift to a greater emphasis on being innovative and being a catalyst of intellectual stimulation and inquiry, harnessing the energy and expertise of all.

Implementing collaborative models such as coteaching engages special and general education teachers collegially to enhance the quality of learning for all students.

There must be a steadfast commitment to making classrooms and the classroom experiences increasingly engaging. Students live and seek to thrive in a world that is increasingly technological. Progressive teaching practices mean the integration and utilization of various technologies.

The new era demands an embrace of virtualization technology that makes teaching and learning environments and schedules more flexible—finally breaking out of the age-old silo model of schools and the cemetery approach to seating order in classrooms. The occurrence of complementary changes and enhancements to professional development make those experiences more relevant and timely.

Preparing for prosperity is about leadership that fosters ambitious organizations, focused on molding the minds and shaping the futures of students. Facilitating the conditions for learning achieves a culture of collaboration and commitment to keen actions. Preparing for prosperity is not an idle intellectual exercise. It is about scrupulous leadership endeavoring to control the institutional destiny.

Chapter Eight

Retooling Schools

Leaders help provide the fertile grounds for the cognitive reaping of the fruit of knowledge.

Positioning for prosperity beckons an answer to the question of "why," lending to the preeminent objective of retooling schools to ensure that the need for change in thinking, pedagogy, and curriculum aligns with and addresses the corollary question of "what" needs to be done. The challenge now becomes making sure rigor, relevance, and relationship in curricula offerings align with pedagogical approaches—"how" teaching occurs with the way students learn.

CONNECTING THE DOTS

The desire to effect change becomes as instrumental as the change itself, and it all hinges upon the culture cultivated and fostered: a culture of high expectations for success by every employee on behalf of and for every student. Preserving the effectiveness and viability of education is about preventing the perpetuation of inequities across buildings—running the gamut from programs, protocols, procedures, pedagogical practices, and methods.

Put simply, continuity is the bottom line, with aligned transitions across levels—elementary, middle school, and high school. Endeavors and initiatives such as vertical and horizontal alignment of curriculum, essential competencies and content, and performance tasks in light of the global challenges faced by students must be a natural evolution of organizational practice.

The administrative capacity, staff adjustments, and program amendments are designed with the end in mind. It is about connecting the dots. The goal is to create a seamless system, focused on capitalizing on all opportunities to positively affect change and progress. Instructional materials are used to create a strong foundation for all students, and ensure that teachers across buildings and grade levels have a common context to instruct students. Clear expectations of accomplishments must be established and embraced, held sacred and mastered.

Consequently, training for the expertise to support these efforts becomes the distinguishing action, giving credence to exceptions only when it is the exception that proves the rule. The use of strategic and systematic goals with corresponding essential objectives must be the guideposts for actions and efforts in the retooling of schools, such as:

Instruction

- Improve student achievement by implementing systematic interventions to respond to student needs: from the provision of academic intervention services, to special education services, to the provision of acceleration and enrichment opportunities
- Improve student achievement by implementing the Common Core Learning Standards K–12. The movement toward a more nationalized curriculum has aided efforts to align what students are taught and better predict the outcome of the educational experience
- Improve student achievement by completing the Annual Professional Performance Review (APPR) and implementing essential components. At the heart of accountability are teachers and administrators alike being prepared and engaged in actions that are steadfastly focused on improving the academic performance of students

Organizational Culture

- Stakeholders are informed and understand district, state, and federal education issues and initiatives. With so many changes afoot, clear communication is vital to help parents and the broader community to be partners in the educational process.
- Foster a districtwide commitment to the physical, social, and emotional safety of students and staff. Schools must be seen as safe havens for learning and development; environments in which the dignity of a student is nourished and preserved.
- Pursue and form new or expanded internal and external partnerships. More and more is being demanded of schools, yet funds are increasingly scarce. Partnerships are key to increasing capacity and preserving options and opportunities for students

Human Resources

- Cultivate an expansive pool of highly qualified and skilled candidates. Schools are human-intensive organizations. Employees are hired to use expertise and skills to enhance the educational experience for students.
- Develop professionals with enhanced capacity to meet the needs of all students. As new and best practices are developed, opportunities for staff to hone and enhance their skills are vital.

Budget and Finance

- Continuous review of programs and operations safeguards cost effectiveness and provides funding opportunities to support program needs and enhancements. The investment in children's education is a societal role and responsibility, and keen fiscal stewardship is the unwavering objective.
- Continuously review and provide for operational support, services, and physical capacity to meet the varied needs of students. Providing quality grounds and facilities, energy efficient systems, safe and dependable pupil transportation, nutritious meals, and technologically equipped buildings serve as the backbone of educational capacity.

The following chart illustrates how the various components connect—from the primary goals to applicable essential objectives:

Mission:
To work continuously and in partnership with the community to ensure that all students develop and demonstrate
the knowledge, skills, abilities and character needed to live useful, productive and rewarding lives.

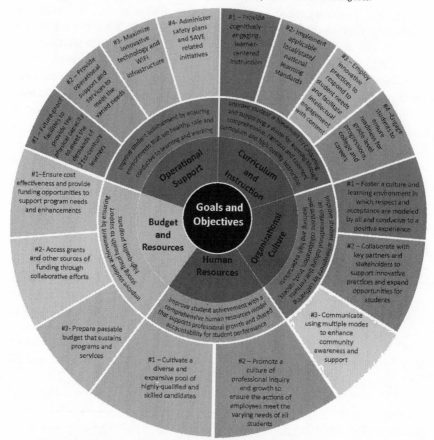

At the heart of it all, the very foundation of instructional leadership is the clear articulation and provision of high-quality K–12 curricula in all academic areas. There must be a retooling of schools to eliminate the silos that hinder substantive change and the formulation of protocols to foster more interdisciplinary opportunities.

To the excitement of some and the chagrin of others, leaders must embrace the reality that education has evolved and will continue to evolve. New norms in curriculum, instruction, and assessment are afoot. Preparing for prosperity means retooling schools by initiating and ultimately institutionalizing multifaceted efforts to respond to student needs. Schools must be committed to preparing students for an ever-changing economy and emerging workforce.

SERVICE FOLLOWS NEEDS

Schools must define essential objectives, effectively implement programs, and ensure that service follows needs. The preservation of the status quo approach can no longer be an acceptable next step. It is about allocating an equitable distribution of services, even at the risk of political sacrifices or offending traditions. The brutish, competitive nature of economics and politics may taint the air, indicating a path of selfish pursuits, but the day is won and the future is preserved by care and compassion: the catalysts for humanistic actions and profoundly positive change. Teachers and administrators who routinely do things that are "above and beyond" the mandates and contractual duties serve to enhance not only educational outcomes but also the educational experience.

Ironically, most often these actions take place quietly behind the scenes without fanfare, recognition, or praise, and without measures that can be neatly quantified. Yes, student test results and teacher/principal evaluation scores help give educators and policymakers a sense of the progress that has been made in relationship to the standards.

However, the reality is that most parents are not concerned about standardized test scores that serve no diagnostic benefit; instead, parents are generally more concerned about a child's learning progress. Subsequently, by having service follow needs, focused on guided independence and helping students be in charge of their own learning, the harsh realities in the worlds of many children can be remarkably changed. The notion of humanity can be revitalized.

The sense of belonging to a community of prosperity reinvigorates and renews the desire to learn, answering the question, what is instrumental to the realization of academic success? So, to ensure progress, there needs to be continued investment, leveraging, and repurposing to bring about quality changes and new implementations.

To that end, there is added emphasis on students' effective navigation of and seamless transitions through the pathways of classes and continuum of services leading to an increased passion for learning. School districts should possess one unified vision, mission, and goal—service following needs in the provision of a quality education for school children.

The charge of preserving the educational welfare of students is embraced with a sense of urgency, devoid of any doubts and skepticism about the commitment to excellence. Service following needs is about leveling the playing field for students; hence some need and deserve more than others in order to ultimately yield similar levels of proficiency over the educational experience.

It is critical to provide research-based Academic Intervention Services (AIS) guided by multiple assessment results (data), focusing on truly enriching the lives of students and moving away from the concept of remediation, which implies that the problem is the child and not the child's experiences. Special education services, for instance, can no longer be about deficits and sympathy but should be provided based on assessment results (data) that are benchmarked against the state standards and appropriately recognize the individual educational needs of each child.

Similarly, the focus on the integration of interactive technology serves to support student learning and allows teachers to truly be facilitators, fostering a thirst for learning. The integration of technology in instruction must serve as an acknowledgment of the reality that the students live in a world of "plug and play" and where there is an "app for that."

EDUCATION IS NOT A SPECTATOR SPORT

Students and educators are inextricably tied, and the tie that binds is the true accountability for students' success. Leadership and learning in school communities must ensure that excellence is the only benchmark for students. Unequivocally and profoundly, the power of education persists; to know is really to succeed. The academic achievement gap has the dubious dichotomous distinction of being caused by and serving as the major driver of social inequality.

Leaders for learning can ill afford to be spectators in the midst of this vortex of change that abounds. The provision of high-quality learning experiences is vitally important.

Education leaders cannot succumb to the otherwise apparently logical ethos of equity and excellence as opposing concepts. It is known that excellence without equity is simply privilege, and equity without excellence is merely tokenism. True excellence in education can only be realized with the absolute manifestation of equity in opportunity.

Education is not at all a spectator sport. It requires a holistic approach that endeavors to turn children on to learning, instilling in them unquenchable appetites to be connoisseurs of knowledge. Every child that experiences an educational system should leave with an extraordinary sense of significance to face an increasingly challenging world with unrelenting resolve and determination.

COMPETING INTERESTS

It is not a question of whether or not school systems will change curricula and instructional focus; it is instead a question of how long will it take to coincide with the knowledge-based economy and the increased pace of information exchange. As the global economy undergoes dramatic changes, schools too must adapt.

The dilemma now, the preeminent leadership challenge, is finding an effective equilibrium amid competing interests within an increasingly stringent fiscal landscape. The changing and emerging workforce environment and the constant barrage of reform efforts presents a series of questions:

- What's the meaning of college and career readiness? Is it merely about providing STEM, CTE, AP, IB, or other career and technical or accelerated programs?
- Are schools structurally (physical settings), organizationally (human capacity), and politically (stakeholder influences) equipped to meet the changing and emerging needs of learners?
- How are the competing interests of standardized testing and assessment effectively balanced with project-based initiatives that garner requisite skills?
- What are those key concrete steps that must be taken?

The bar has been raised; consequently, the leadership challenge must be embraced. The need for schools to be key partners in workforce strategic initiatives, for instance, has taken on an increased sense of immediacy since society is more and more preoccupied with the value of the marketplace and financial portfolios than the value of the life of the child. The role and involvement of public schools helps to balance the dominance of profit-motivated megamergers and the one-size-fits-all approach.

To that end, public schools stand as the linchpin to the revitalization and stabilization of the economy and even the nation's emergence as a technology superpower. While it is important that partnerships and collaborations concentrate on realizing economic gains, it is vitally important to give all students an individual sense of significance. Children from poor and urban communities in which the feeling of competence has significantly eroded and a viable shot of making dreams a prosperous reality has been fleeting are vulnerable.

No longer can certain segments of society be systematically isolated from being partakers of high-end jobs and higher educational pursuits. This era of excellence compels the asking and the answering of the question, "What is done when it is known that children are barely or not realizing their potential?" Inasmuch as failure is not an option, success is required. Schools and educators fail when the children fail.

Therefore, acting as reasonable parents do is the norm; recognizing that it is not always done right but the objective is to never cease in attempting to get it right. The more the potential in students is recognized, even when that potential is not yet fully developed, the more doors are opened to progress through the educational system. Ultimately, the performance of educator is defined by the excellence derived from students.

CONSTANCY IN PURPOSE

The charge of the profession compels actions focused on alleviating the barriers to excellence in learning and in performance. Thought leaders are duty-bound to approach every day and every experience as the proving grounds of ingenuity by possessing laser-sharp constancy in purpose. Every decision, every action taken, is focused on doing what is right.

The constancy in purpose is derived from the profound belief that children depend on and deserve the best of good intentions. Schools must systematically, environmentally, and culturally commit to the academic needs of every child. It is a cohesive shift of the educational paradigm to educating all students at a high level of proficiency.

No longer can there be acceptable losses. A failing child becomes an adult who will struggle and be a burden, not a benefit, to society. Fundamentally, success for all must become the mantra and the driving force for progressive change. A vibrant and real commitment to excellence is in order, necessitating a steadfast focus on continuous improvement, which could vary and be interpreted differently based on perspective and positional authority.

At the heart of any continuous improvement effort must be the goal of enhancing capacity so that instruction and accountability for student performance is the priority. That fundamental tenet transcends the varied perspectives and serves to center discussions and decisions. Efforts translate into engaging and supporting a tripartite model:

- Standardization of what is taught: curriculum/essential content and competencies; state and federal standards
- Consistency in how it is taught: instruction and methodology; academic intervention supports
- Predictability of successful performance: assessment through standardized tests and report cards; progress monitoring to influence success

A quality education or schooling is about application of the content: ELA—comprehension and drawing inferences; math/science—analysis and data mining to refine problems and change reality, not simply to solve a formula; social studies—historical context for current events to help forecast future eventualities; languages other than English—appreciation of the nuances of different cultures.

Congruently, constancy in purpose is about fostering and sustaining school and district climates that are conducive to effective teaching and learning. Structural changes provide the requisite capacity to:

- effectively monitor student and teacher performance to ensure continuous growth and improvement
- analyze diagnostic data on an on-going basis—moving away from sole reliance on postmortem data from state and/or federal agencies
- vertically and horizontally aligning programs and services across buildings or within buildings—standardization

Subsequently, discrete steps must be employed:

- leveling the workload and providing for realistic expectations for accountability
- standardizing processes, directing specific procedures while preserving the freedom to create and innovate, and recognition of the art and the science of pedagogy
- creating clear expectations of performance, a focus on quality
- effectively evaluating actual performance—data might measure results, but it does not reveal the details of the actual process being followed every day and focused on the learning outcome
- facilitating thorough decision making, hence sustaining progress
- involving various stakeholders in shared decision making and consensus building
- clarifying lines of authority and accountability, and coordinating efforts to yield more expedient implementations
- promoting greater awareness of the overall district mission by students, faculty and staff, parents, and the community
- supporting continuous flow in long-range instructional planning via a backward-design process based on a profile of a graduate; providing students what is needed, when it is needed, and in the most appropriate way
- linking practices, procedures, curriculum, program offerings, assessments, and evaluation of performance
- identifying problems early and expediting corrective actions, moving away from current trends of using postmortem data (attacking a problem about a child way after the fact, if directly at all)
- filtering out repetitive processes; working smarter, more productively, and avoiding the frustration of being extremely busy with limited gains for efforts rendered
- keeping each school building, each department, each classroom, and the district as a whole focused on the value-added nature of the educational experience and effectively gauging progress along the way

Constancy of purpose is possible only after the stabilization and standard-ization of processes, procedures, protocols, programs, and provisions—all the conditions for learning. The formula calls for an organizational structure that is built on the premise that curriculum and instruction are at the core of the district's mission.

There must be an individual and collective embrace of change as the catalyst for progress. Staff development must be strategically targeted to bolster and fuel the manifestation of articulated goals. The hope, the vision, and subsequent actions must be focused on enriching the experience for all children, from those who are lagging to those who are accelerated beyond their years.

Chapter Nine

Convert Challenges into Opportunities

> The clout of the passionate individual is being motivated by principle and driven by equal parts of dissatisfaction and idealism . . . ordinary people driven to do extraordinary things to correct an obvious wrong.

Public education has stood the test of time, serving as a conduit for prosperity. However, public education is at the proverbial fork in the road, faced with multiple and often competing demands. Essentially, the prevailing winds of change that have been expected are upon us. Over the past decade, the changes have been unprecedented and historical.

The abounding challenges also present as opportunities, each needing the other to exist. As the adage states, "Only scarred hands can heal," meaning that opposition and challenge are prerequisites for success. In the same manner, dissent and opposition are vital to change and advancement.

The transformation of challenges into opportunities means defining and redefining new norms of proficiency, new norms of pedagogy, and new norms for performance. The challenges include the changing demographics and need to respect diversity, new understandings about learning and assessments, proliferation of technology, and the ebbs and flows of finances. The environment is ripe and riddled with competing and contradictory attempts of reform and reification, ranging from politics to idealism.

The once assured bright future, the hallmark destiny of public education, is in serious jeopardy. As a result, educators across the nation are rightfully angry and feel under attack. Schools have entered into a tailspin, with one challenge after another. The volume of the acidic rhetoric has become too loud to ignore.

Approaching the qualms of an aggressive reform agenda calls for a bold embrace of the challenges while endeavoring to transform them into educationally stimulating and relevant experiences for students. It is hard work. It is work compelling persistence and an unwavering sense of determination. It is work that spurs an internally optimistic perspective to transform the challenges into opportunities. The time is ripe for a reflective pause, to give a little pep talk and be reminded of the common charge of challenging each and every opportunity to do things even better.

The dueling yet complimentary concepts of challenges and opportunities dictate that action be taken. "Iron sharpens iron" means that when faced with the most challenging situation or circumstances it is about pushing harder to be even better—honing skills. It is critical that the focus remains on the mission—students and their educational welfare.

Institutions of learning literally and figuratively stand as islands of hope in the sea of dreams for all the students. Ultimately, the end result is cementing an unwavering commitment to be the staunchest advocates for the preservation of a world-class education for every student. A keen scrutiny of the complexities of education, defined by punctuated unpredictability and the immense emergence of new knowledge, effectively illustrates that only those who still possess a pure sense of idealism can truly and honestly redefine the social norms.

In the same way the old adage of "teach effectively and the scores will come" is prophetic, so is the command that lead keenly and challenges will be transformed. It is about teachers of teachers and leaders of leaders dissecting and analyzing critical issues in education from varied perspectives, fervently using data to substantiate beliefs, the highest ideals of teaching and learning.

EDUCATIONAL SPECTRUM: GOING FROM HERE TO THERE

Despite the pungency of the challenges, leaders must also see beyond them, grasping the goal of progressiveness. The mindsets of educators can no longer be fixed, looking only from a singular perspective, or worse, from a rearview vantage point, only concerned about the past or perseverating on the challenges. There must be a commitment to make the shift, to cultivate learning to meet the continuously changing demands for present and future students. Education must be stayed on meeting children where they are, acknowledging their reality.

In thinking about the current status and condition of education and contemplating future direction and next steps, it all starts with the simple recognition that education is evolving. When viewed from an ecological perspective, it is clear and evident that the educational spectrum is changing, some aspects faster than others.

To that end, the focus must be on cultivating learning to better meet the emerging demands students face. Think about it for a moment: children entering kindergarten in 2017 are members of the Class of 2030, and kids born in 2017 will be members of the class of 2035. The world will be a lot different and demand a lot more from them than it does now. The reality is that the kindergartners of fifteen years ago, the high school or college gradu-ates of today, could not imagine a workforce affixed with opportunities in nanotechnology.

Similarly, kindergartners of today will someday embark upon a world in which the types of jobs have yet to be conceived, much less designed. The consolation is the uncertainty and changing futures of students stimulate a shared compulsion to create a world-class workforce, bonding education and business in a common quest. The confounding nature of the workforce with varying demands has shown the spotlight on and cemented broad interest in the influence and impact of education.

The result is an altering of perspective for educational systems, demand-ing both an individual and a collective commitment to ensure all students meet and exceed increasingly higher benchmarks and expectations. Global competiveness has markedly influenced the marketplace, consequently im-pacting the educational arena. It is exceedingly clear that the tapestry of societal boundaries has been rendered pervasively seamless with human be-ings from every corner of the globe becoming more intertwined with each other in economic, political, and cultural arenas.

Regardless of race, creed, religion, socioeconomic circumstance, or abil-ity, students must be prepared to thrive in a global marketplace with an understanding and appreciation of the multicultural context. As advanced technologies and communications bring the world's communities closer, the educational spectrum shifts even more so.

PRISONERS OF PAST ASSUMPTIONS

Educators are the people who best internalize the understanding that the things that are most notable were once deemed impossible; hence it is essen-tial to possess a sincere passion for what is possible. It is vital that innovative minds are not prisoners of past assumptions; that they not succumb to the age-old practice of trying to solve tomorrow's problems with yesterday's solutions.

A shift in assumptions is about people and practices. There must be a steadfast focus on hiring highly skilled, competent, and appropriately creden-tialed personnel that reflect the current needs and demands, demographics, and vision for future endeavors; or, provide extensive and intensive training to foster an open-competitive mindset to organizational effectiveness. Schools across the nation are hyperfocused on high-stakes testing with in-creased rigor and expectations for performance.

Inasmuch as that is the case, the matter of the world being flat begs the question about the assumptions made about educating all kids versus educating some, while simply training numerous others for minimal-paying entry-level jobs. The true role of public schools comes under scrutiny. Do past assumptions still stand? Should a child who walks in the door of a school building as a kindergartner with minimal literacy exposure, who in a year enhances literacy or numeracy skills tenfold but still falls below testing standards, be deemed unsuccessful? Should that school be branded as a failing institution?

Or, should a child speaking little or no English, with little or no formal education, who in three years is proficient in English but did not realize the passing benchmark on a state assessment be deemed a failure? What is truly the role of public schools? What are the assumptions about success or failure? These questions exemplify the crux of the matter; the incarcerating effect current models and messaging about academic growth have had on an increasingly growing population of students.

Take the pathological effects of poverty that depress the aspirations of students. The reality of poor students is not so much about money in the pure sense of cash reserves. It is about adequate access to nutritious foods, inadequate housing and medical care, or the overall lack of a true sense of significance in a society filled with waste and wealth. With those mounting challenges comes the opportunity to shift the paradigm for teacher training and subsequently pedagogy.

It would be invaluable to require that all preservice education programs include a career-based internship outside of student teaching so teachers can have, at a minimum, a superficial awareness of the harsh realities of the marketplace in which students aspire and endeavor upon graduation. In the same way a medical doctor is not thrust into a wide variety of live/actual situations and environments before completing residency rounds, wide exposure and ultimate specialization should be the norm for teachers and administrators.

The current model, with the predominance of teacher placements in suburban schools and viewing urban placements as the exceptional option, perpetuates the middle-class mindset. When juxtaposed against an increasingly diverse student population, such a perspective is warped and compounds the matter. How would that teacher see and interact with students differently? Would that teacher possess a more laserlike focus on doing whatever it takes to help children learn, breaking the mental chains of bondage that perpetuate generational poverty and undereducation? Not only do teachers need to be made aware of the salient issues, real counteractive and remedial strategies are to be provided and mastered.

As the educational landscape is redefined by the diversity of learners and as traditional means for learning are falling short, the challenge of complexity becomes the opportunity for authenticity. Instead of repackaging the old in hope of yielding a different result (insanity), the heightened exposure to the unique needs of students provides the opportunity to better personalize the learning experience. Teachers, novice and veterans alike, must be entrenched in training and real exposures about the significant realities of children of poverty, English as New Language Learners (ENL), underachieving learners, and special education students.

Correspondingly, there must be a measured demonstration to ensure proficiency in performance for all students, recognizing that the aspirational goal is the mastery level. K–12 schools should focus on helping students build strong skills and develop insatiable appetites for learning new things. Will the status quo be revered and rendered, with children continuing to be prisoners of past assumptions? Preparation is warranted for schools to transform the evolving challenges into glorious opportunities.

FACILITATING LEARNING

As such, pedagogy in school districts has been enhanced due to the plethora of research on how the brain works and how students learn. Discoveries in neuroscience and psychology have provided new insights on thinking and the application to learning. School leaders are keenly aware of the various learning styles and the need to focus teaching and learning on critical thinking, problem solving, and contextual learning skills through targeted staff development initiatives.

Teaching has shifted from the days of teachers simply assigning, monitoring, and correcting. Educators are expected to be facilitators of learning, shifting the instructional focus to a greater emphasis on innovating as the catalyst of intellectual stimulation and inquiry. Engaging and maximizing instructional technology, facilitating learning via online platforms, virtual field trips, intercontinental connections, constructed project-based approaches—all must become second nature in public schools, embedded in the fabric of program provisions.

Ultimately, the true measure of schools rests with the success of all students and not merely those that society expects to be successful because of the circumstances of birth. Many highly talented students fail or drop out of school as a result of the disconnection of the required demonstrations of learning and multiplicity of students' learning styles. Consequently, the fundamental premise of leadership is to facilitate the effective use of what is learned rather than just stockpile information.

Many students are being asked to demonstrate knowledge in ways totally unrelated to how they learn, which often hinges upon enculturation. A child, for instance, with the capacity to write and recite complex lyrics for a rap song is left incapacitated by structures requiring the expression of content understanding in traditional ways. Or, a child with writing dexterity limits stemming from dyslexia is rendered incompetent due to illegible writing, not reflective of course mastery.

Schools need to be much more limber in changing with the times, not only in the context of what is being taught but also how students are being taught and assessed. The prerequisite for educators is to work in concert and construct learning communities, whether it is through multidisciplinary projects, technological integration, globally based lesson planning, or differentiated instruction. Facilitating learning is about fertilizing skills and attributes that support continuous learning.

The very notion that all students follow a similar course progression and take the same battery of tests to graduate runs counter to aligning K–12 efforts with a wide variety of college majors or career skills, much less the illimitable virtual classroom and learning opportunities that exist. Schools systems of tomorrow must out-innovate in order to out-compete and keep the critics at bay.

DIGITAL NATIVES

Students of today are digital natives, born into a world in which advanced technology is second nature, placing an evolving dilemma at the feet of education leaders. The effectiveness and relevance of practices, along with the definition and expectation of success, are called in question. The goal is to ensure schools are equipped to help students hone the requisite skills to be competitive at the next level and are not stifled by traditional structures and expectations.

Students live and seek to thrive in a world that is increasingly technological. The engagement with technology isn't so much about the technological tools as it is about the learning possibilities those tools provide. Investing heavily in the integration of technology in support of academic retooling must be a mainstay. Environments must be cultivated and staff trained to enable wireless technology and hand-held devices to flourish for enhanced academic outcomes and pursuits, rendering schools boundless and unearthing limitless opportunities for students.

With the rapid proliferation of instructional software, there must be a commitment to invest in instructional materials that are engaging, dynamic, and responsive to informational changes. Key and strategic capital investments must be made to ensure ubiquitous access- reliable Wi-Fi access everywhere, and modernized learning spaces, which enable seamless use of mobile devices, providing a continuum of innovative and differentiated approaches, opportunities, programs, and services.

For instance, revelations from the simplest logistics of seating configurations in the typical classroom call into question the effectiveness of traditional practices in the face of increased knowledge about complex aspects of learning styles. The higher expectation and added attention given to students when sitting in the front of the room often yields a higher level of engagement, focus, and less temptation or distraction by other stimuli. That being the case, a student's lack of mastery cannot be the result of simple logistics of a seating chart. There will always be a back of the room, and there will always be those who choose to sit there. Subsequently, the key is educators making the adjustments in delivery systems, such as the engagement with and the maximization of instructional technology.

While technology is not the cure all, it is a vehicle to help shift the instructional paradigm. The predominant focus should be formulating learning communities that allow progressive program offerings that employ much more engaging and interactive methodologies and practices.

Embarking on initiatives such as Bring Your Own Device (BYOD)—an invitation to students to bring a device if the teacher, parents, and student believe it would be useful to support the learning process—should be the accepted policy and the not the exception to the policy.

The focus is not so much on technology itself but on how technology is used to satisfy the learning pallets of digital natives. Educators play a vital role in connecting the "3 Rs—Reading, Writing, and (A)rithmetic"—with the "4 Cs—Critical thinking, Communication, Collaboration, and Creativity." Online and virtual classroom spaces must be supported and become more prevalent.

To make learning relevant and rigorous, students should be provided with a variety of experiences and exposures, some of which are linked directly to local business and updated regularly to align with workforce development perspectives. Classes that operate in virtual space and maximize cloud computing should be the norm and not the celebrated exception. Allow students more access to core academic credit through relevant Career Technology Education (CTE), curricula that are relevant to college or career interest or aspirations.

The very notion of the traditional teacher has been redefined and re-normed to be someone adept in instructional technology, fluent in social network vocabulary, and liberal in the embrace of change. It behooves school leaders and districts to support endeavors that focus on blending technology with traditional pedagogy. Permission to engage in charting new paths and redefining norms must be granted in order to emancipate from the shackles of the past.

INVESTMENT NOT AN EXPENSE

The "perfect storm" has brewed and overflowed in schools across the country. The notion that the greatest investment a society can make is the investment in the future of children—education—has taken a back burner to special interest and fortification of wealthy corporate structures. Education must become the "first dollar" invested and not be viewed as a fiscal burden.

Purveyors of privatizing education are bent on spewing anonymous vitriol aimed at making the access to a quality public education irrelevant by depicting it as an expense. The advantages and benefits once viewed as a given for educators are being strategically depleted by political chicanery and unfunded ideals. Politicians look good, children and schools get the short end, and taxpayers are left holding the bag, footing the bill. Governors and state legislators are not as keen to support schools with appropriate state aid, even when there is clear evidence that states' investments in public schools are below the constitutional level of providing a sound basic education.

The fiscal crisis has seeped into the reality of daily living and discussions when coupled with the increasing demands placed on schools; it is even more challenging to preserve high-quality programs and services. For the foreseeable future, school districts will experience financial hemorrhaging, and students will be faced with significant increases in class sizes, major reductions in extracurricular offerings, and little to no access to engage in project-based, experiential learning opportunities.

How long can schools sustain quality when for the past several years the solution to budget dilemmas has been program cuts? The need to cultivate learning compels the need for an entrepreneurial perspective: effectively and efficiently meeting the demands of the time, now and into the future. The rough currents of shrinking coffers establish the ultimatum of making difficult decisions and implementing ways to weather the fiscal storms. Efforts must be driven by a value-added focus knowing that investments and actions today will define the trajectory for students' success.

Investments in learning must be leveraged through strategic actions such as future-proofing facilities, modernizing to not only meet existing needs but also needs on the outer horizon. Further still, there needs to be a continued investment in accountability-implementing comprehensive evaluation processes without eroding production. There must be deliberate efforts to form partnerships to support and enhance capacity, steadfastly focused on exposing students to emerging opportunities.

In the long run, fiscal leadership is not simply about reductions and balancing a budget. It is about vision and upholding the integrity of the commitment to provide quality programs and services to children. Both short- and long-term structural changes to the financing and support education service delivery models are needed. There must be an allowance for flexibility, enabling schools to be agile enough to make the key changes and leverage opportunities.

Solutions to help fill funding gaps in the K–12 arena readily are prevalent, from simple alternative funding measures such as revenue generated from advertisement on district websites, to corporate sponsorships of facilities or corporate seed funding for specific programs, to more complex relationships such as regional consortiums of school districts.

Incentivizing private/public consortiums by the state, either through direct startup funding or flexible aid reimbursements, will undoubtedly maximize economies of scope and scale within schools and communities. Such allowances are an investment in the congruence among districts: programs, processes, models, policies, regulations, support structures, culture, communication, partnerships, and finances.

The identification of the collective pool and deciphering of how to best leverage opportunities ensures the provision and sustaining of a rigorous and comprehensive continuum of services and instructional options. Essentially, the richness of the educational experience for both students and educators alike is enhanced by the provision of interdisciplinary opportunities.

Leadership in these harsh fiscal times must be committed to certain guiding principles:

- Value Added: Raising achievement and improving operations
- Cost Effectiveness: Doing things more effectively and efficiently, balancing lower costs without jeopardizing program quality
- Tax Impact Sensitivity: Multiple-year analysis of tax levies and rates and trend analysis of property valuations

An objective assessment of current conditions and desired outcomes is required. Decisions to fund certain programs or personnel come only after careful analysis of alternatives.

School districts' budget decisions are not made in isolation and are not politically motivated, but instead are rendered as a part of a data-driven school improvement effort. Resources properly placed yield opportunities to improve the performance of students. A fiscal crisis beckons aggressive and strategic plans, focused on:

- Avoiding scenarios where educational quality is negative
- Educating political leaders of the impact of politically sensational decisions
- Requiring an increased commitment by all school personnel to help reduce costs, and
- Informing the public of the problem and the reliance on greater support of schools

As such, schools must engage in multiyear financial forecasts and planning:

- Assessing the sustainability of bargaining unit contracts to preserve staff
- Analyzing benefit trends (contribution levels, co-pays, self-funding options for health insurance and drug plans)
- Studying Facilities—enabling schools to maximize the tremendous possibilities of emerging technology

Similarly, the times require the formation of consortiums that connect colleges, local business, and secondary schools, consequently providing:

- Access to professionals and experts in the field that is being taught
- Relevance to various career fields
- Access to equipment and facilities that are cost prohibitive for local schools
- Internships for students and externships for educators

It is critical that investments are made in areas of strength while making strategic realignments in areas of need. As such, budget deliberations are focused on cost containment and increased efficiency. The end goal is to balance finances without adversely impacting the quality of education; in fact, improving upon the quality of education.

Even in these harshest economic and political times, the quality of K–12 and higher education remains an attraction point. Parents still have one common goal, a quality education for their children. Consequently, educators must remain steadfast and committed to giving students concrete reasons to succeed.

Schools must be committed to making classrooms and the classroom experience increasingly interesting and engaging; leveraging resources to provide equipment, staff development, and infrastructure at a time when funds are hard to come by. The reality for many schools, however, looms on being grimmer considering that many school leaders are not educated in finance or school business management.

By taking the perspective that fiscal leadership is about emphasizing and investing in improving instruction for quality student achievement, a lack of specific knowledge can be neutralized. The plausibility of loss of countless nights of sleep contemplating how to best preserve core programs in the face of increasingly shrinking resources, and the anxiety about the shifts in the Common Core, are eradicated by acceptance of the premise that education is an investment.

Shrinking funds are not an excuse for schools to shirk on their mission to prepare students with the skill sets for the twenty-first-century marketplace and the increased competitiveness of a global society defined by rapid technological advancements. Subsequently, school systems must become even more resolute in the commitment to provide a continuum of effective approaches, opportunities, programs, and services that embrace learning as fundamental.

Whatever the angst—increased rigor of assessments, the evolving roles and responsibilities, or even the outcomes of evaluation systems that assign scores and ratings to teachers and principals—a shift in perspective helps to convert challenges into opportunities.

Chapter Ten

The Horizon Leans Forward

Life at its best is the creative synthesis of opposites; in other words, you are at your best when you are assertive in your pursuits yet humble in the afterglow of your achievement.

Historically people have experienced and embraced a series of interrelated changes in thinking and behaving. From slavery to civil rights, industrialization and urbanization, revolutions in transportation and communication, the Internet and globalization of business and commerce all served as catalysts, challenging social norms of thinking and acting.

Looking toward the horizon, in the midst of fiscal uncertainty, the focus of school districts must be on preserving quality programs for students. The arc to a brighter future compels a passionate belief in students' capacity to achieve, and reinforcement of the talent and capability to achieve at the highest levels. These are the crucial moments in which leaders embrace the challenge, inspiring and motivating a sense of passion, a sense of commitment, and a sense of urgency to learn.

Simply put, astute leadership renders the removal of contradictions; what is believed to be quality educational opportunities and the realities of challenges schools face as manifested in the performance of students. Consequently, such actions epitomize the belief that the obligations of educators are not met until all students are performing at peak potential, ready to embrace life's many challenges. In essence, educators have an individual and a collective obligation to help students succeed and forge ahead.

Through education students learn to appreciate that life is about resiliency and the willingness to endure the ebbs and flows. School systems hold the promise of a brighter tomorrow. Through effective and potent leadership the American Dream for every child is reclaimed and seized. The imagination is held as the only limitation, cementing the belief that a student's place is anywhere dreams take them. Educators give wings to dreams and help bring students to their preferred futures. When it is all said and done, the dreams and hopes of children must beat in their hearts and souls, constantly being reminded that good, better, best, never let it rest, until good is better and better is best.

EDUCATION IS A CIVIL RIGHT

The staunch advocacy of education as a civil right is critical for the educational vitality of countless students. The conviction that education of and for all children is a moral mandate for a civil society must be sacrosanct. Of all the civil rights for which the world has struggled and fought, the right to learn is undoubtedly the most fundamental.

Justice Thurgood Marshall's 1974 dissenting opinion in *Milliken v. Bradley* (a 5 to 4 Supreme Court ruling) sums it up best:

> We deal here with the right of all our children, whatever their race, to an equal start in life and to an equal opportunity to reach their full potential as citizens. Those children who have been denied that right in the past deserve better than to see fences thrown up to deny them that right in the future. Unless our children begin to learn together, there is little hope that our people will ever learn to live together.

The freedom to learn compels demonstration of the resolve to go from failure to failure without losing enthusiasm. The freedom to learn compels the expansion of circumstances to fit big dreams. The freedom to learn compels the determination to be zealous in the face of challenge and adversity. The freedom to learn compels the avoidance of derailing or deferring dreams because of baseless pride and unabashed arrogance. The freedom to learn compels not stopping at rejection, if the goal is to get to reward. The freedom to learn has been purchased with bitter sacrifice.

An informed and principled mission to ensure the vitality of a quality education for all children in every school district, in every corner of the state and country, should not be optional. The power of education is not only transformational and transcending for the individual student, it is multigenerational. It is widely documented that the success of a child, or lack thereof, not only paves the way or prohibits success into adulthood, it also serves to cement the beliefs and values parlayed from one generation to the next.

Vigilance and hopefulness are key ingredients to long-term and lasting positive impact on the lives of children. The question now is how hopefulness converts into practices that address the increasing achievement gaps between subsections of the student population.

The nation's persistent racial inequalities show up particularly clearly in schools. Unequal educational opportunity stands as the roadblock to equal life chances and full, equal citizenship. Inequalities in education are a reflection of larger inequalities that exist in every segment of American society.

The problems faced are multifaceted and stem from a variety of tangled forces. A complete shift of the paradigm and a thorough review and modification of long-standing processes and protocols is called for. Leading for second-order change, however, will undoubtedly take a great personal toll, exemplifying why so many promising practices in education never lead to improved student achievement. Standing up for a position and being attacked reinforces that standing up is necessary.

CHASMS IN PERFORMANCE

It is not by happenstance that states across the nation, complying with applicable laws, rules, and regulations, are publishing "failing" schools lists that are overwhelmingly segregated by poverty and race. It is not ironic or coincidental that the US rate of incarceration is five to eight times higher than other highly developed countries, and black males are the largest percentage of inmates. The unfortunate reality is that organizations are designed to get the results realized.

The Children's Defense Fund has identified it as America's "School to Prison Pipeline" that only results in shattered lives and extinguished dreams. Increasingly, states across the country are using statistics of proficiency or the lack thereof on third- and fourth-grade tests to help forecast the number of prisons to be constructed. So much for "No Child Left Behind."

The epidemic that faces this and future generations of poor, black, and Latino youths are so invasive and pervasive that scholars have coined phrases to vividly describe the phenomena. It is said that nationally, poor, black, and Latino youths are suffering from internal political efficacy. In other words, there exists general and routine self-doubt about the ability to be appreciated as a contributing member of society.

Congruently, there is an abundant manifestation of the signs and symptoms of external political efficacy. Too many adolescents believe that even if they were to try to make a positive contribution, society would not allow them to do so or would at least put up impediments to progress. Hence, "giving up" and "stop trying" become acceptable alternatives.

This type of pervasive malcontent is unfortunately consistent with the words professed by Dr. King in his 1956 speech, "Desegregation and the Future." According to Dr. King,

> We must face the tragic fact that we are far from the promised land in the struggle for a desegregated society. Segregation is still a glaring fact in Ameri-

ca. History has proven that social systems have a great last minute breathing power and the guardians of the status quo are always on hand with their oxygen tanks to keep the old order alive.

After more than a half century since the landmark *Brown v. Board of Education* decision, questions still linger about the realization of the dreams and hopes of education as an inevitable civil right. It seems only reasonable and logical for one to surmise that every black and brown child in America would be basking in the sweet afterglow of equity and equality of education.

Instead the achievement gap between minority students and white students persists as one of the nation's most pressing social problems. It is not just access to education or schooling but access to experiences, in and outside of school, that foster and facilitate critical thinking and reflective learning in preparation for a knowledge-driven, global marketplace.

Oftentimes it is not because certain students are less capable that they don't realize academic benchmarks. It is more so a function of being utterly disabled by the lack of adequate supports and real attention to students' unique needs. The real culprit is an unfair, unjust, and simply immoral system that has been perpetuated and has yielded greater inequities and inequalities in public school systems.

Increasingly so, poor, black, and Latino students are considerably more than likely to have uncertified teachers in core academic subjects, attend schools that are in poor condition, and are often stigmatized by the unfortunate socioeconomic circumstances of birth. And disproportionality, disparities in performance parallel the lines of special education classifications. The gap in academic achievement is not the problem. It is merely a manifestation of too many false promises and failed policies. It is indeed a symptom of gross disparities in communities.

Far too many children are victims of their parents' craziness (bad decisions) and of the unfortunate circumstances of birth. The pernicious effects of poor education in many schools are symptomatic of the incongruity of the manifestation of the democratic ideal with the plight of persons of color and the poor. An achievement gap separating black from white students has long been documented—a social divide extremely vexing to policymakers and the target of one blast of school reform after another.

The story of the education gap that is being told is one sided, and what is occluded is more significant than what is being sensationalized, or oversimplified. What about the realities that schools attended by poor black children have historically been underfunded and are ill stocked with high-quality professionals? What about the significant realities that ENL and special education students are largely precluded from the rosters of charter schools? What about the profit motive and who gains from public funding of private entities? What about simple sustainability of privatization when local control is wrenched away?

Schools have much more to contend with than what is being sensationalized and oversimplified. The struggles in schools stem from the complex manifestation of economic deprivation, psychological manipulation, intellectual malnutrition, and cultural disenfranchisement within society, all of which are the sources of self-doubt and destruction. The chasm in the performance gap has produced a two-tier education system that is being increasingly exacerbated by access to technology.

Society can ill afford to have chasms in performance signified by the technological haves and the have-nots. The economically disadvantaged in comparison to the quintessential middle-class student who popularizes the success columns in school profile reports must be equalized through enhanced performance for all students. The astonishing gaps in performance and the spiraling denial of quality education to all kids, regardless of the walk of life, is a stern challenge to democracy.

Literacy is a necessity for full involvement in a democratic society. The inevitable consequence of illiteracy is marginalization, a portion of the public school population being unable to effectively compete in the global marketplace. Even for the most menial low-paying jobs, solid literacy, numeracy, and technological proficiency are required.

CALL IN THE WILDERNESS

There is a tremendous need for much greater diversity in leadership positions, across all industries, and most notably in public education systems because of the visibility and tangibility of these positions of power as models for students. Schools play a vital role in addressing the imperative of inequity and inequality that has spun a web of disillusionment, disappointment, deferral, and despair.

Countless adults and children are psychologically and financially trapped in an airtight cage of poverty, allocated to the realm of the social underclass and deemed as insignificant in the social hierarchy. The societal psychosis promotes a battlefield encompassing mental chains of bondage—the ingrained attitude or repression, of subsumed subservience and servitude, of entitlement superiority, and of racist and discriminate systems and principalities.

Leading for learning in a diverse world is highly essential to eradicating the "What difference would it make, anyway?" type of attitude that has dispirited, depressed, and disabled too many students. Far too many have been rendered with staunch cynicism, disillusionment, and withdrawal. In that vein diverse leadership and leadership with a diverse perspective is a necessity for continued progress. It pleas for reconstituting, revitalizing, and reinforcing the one institution that made the American dream a reality for tens of millions, access to a quality education.

Race and race relations define the DNA of human history, and that DNA blueprint stipulates that existence of diversity. While so, the DNA construct also stipulates inextricable ties as human beings. The manifestation of a dual society brought on by injustice must be stricken, rendering differences as strengths and not as weaknesses. The most immoral act is to do nothing in the face of injustice. This is witnessed when leadership succumbs to the subtle, psychological techniques employed in this contemporary day of political correctness and expediency, superficial liberalism, and conservative pluralism.

No longer can shortsighted behaviors, motivated by the desire for instant gratification or social or political acceptance, be allowed to dictate actions and decision. Yielding to such actions only comes at the expense of future rewards. There is a cry in the wilderness for diverse leadership and leadership with a diverse perspective in an increasingly diverse world—leadership that will be truthful, spiritual, and sincere. It is time for leaders with a true sense of morality, who are cognizant of implicit biases and subconscious discriminatory traits that support the assumption of a role on the sidelines watching the compilation of mountains of injustice.

The courageous will to cut off the chains of hate and push open freedom's gate ensures that every child, regardless of zip code of residency, has a quality education. As Dr. King so eloquently but poignantly outlined, "Inferior education, poor housing, unemployment, and inadequate health care stand as the bitter components of oppression, the ultimate annihilator of dreams and hopes." This sounds all too familiar, the promises made on presidential campaign trails.

There is a need, now more than ever, for leadership that is tough minded enough to break the mental chains of prejudice, half-truths, stereotypes, and ignorance. However, there has been an avoidance of real action. Far too much vacillation, genuflecting, and procrastination on the issues of social injustice, inequity, and inequality have been witnessed. Education leaders must work tirelessly and relentlessly to be the trailblazers of human, academic, scientific, and religious freedom and justice.

It is indeed up to educators to transfix and transform America's greatest dilemma into her most glorious opportunity. It is incumbent on leaders to abhor racism, sexism, and all the other "isms" and "schisms" that prevent harmonious living, fostering a spirit of cooperation rather than the divisiveness of the spirit of competition. More and more as a nation there is a preoccupation about and with weapons of mass destruction, while increasingly ignoring the weapons of mass self-destruction: drug addiction, obesity, sexually transmitted diseases, teen pregnancy, and high school dropout.

Those are the pathological behaviors that stem from educational skill gaps, structural unemployment, institutionalized racism, welfare dependency, and broken homes.

There is a pervasive and insidious development of alienation in this contemporary society, degrading the fabric of social culture and social systems. Many communities and public school systems are now more segregated than in the days before desegregation. Schools stand at the proverbial crossroads in society. Through education, students, the next generation of leaders, are reminded that the differences that define the people of a nation can never be deemed as a deficit or a means for deteriorating the human spirit. The strength of diversity must instead be deemed as the glue that binds all together as one nation.

The strength of America is intrinsically meshed in the active participation of all the people. For that reason it must be made clear that being a productive and contributing citizen of this society is not a spectator sport; it is an educational prerogative. Being an informed, responsible, and active participant amid this vortex of change is an inherent responsibility in a democratic political society.

There is a call in the wilderness for an evolutionary revolution. There is a call for changing systems, cultures, and institutionalized modus operandi. The answer to the call requires a wholehearted commitment to maximizing economic and political opportunities for all students, and not just those who fit the quintessential middle-class model. There must be a steadfast focus on the advancement of education for all students.

Fundamental change is needed in how poverty and the penetrating pains of institutional racism are viewed and contended with. Simply look at the makeup of prisons versus colleges. Penitentiaries and correctional facilities have unfortunately become a mainstay for the undereducated and those suffering from mental health issues. Lockup and not academia is a rite of passage for far too many children. The possibility to matriculate in college is a fleeting reality.

Is it happenstance or design? It is vital that leaders for learning commit to the betterment of all the children and answer the call in the wilderness.

LOOK BACK TO LOOK AHEAD

As the African proverb dictates, "Each one must teach one." Each generation has a responsibility to ensure that the preceding generation is better off as a result of the legacy left behind by the previous generation. In essence, educators have an individual and a collective obligation to help students succeed and forge ahead. A quality education is the preservation of legacy, for it is not the remembered past but the forgotten past that enslaves and perpetuates negativities.

Leaders for learning now need to seize the chance to make the difficulties worthwhile. Positioned at proverbial crossroads, precariously teetering on the precipice of prosperity, leaders are compelled to undergo serious soul search-ing, knowing that oftentimes it is not the enemy out there that is most con-cerning but instead the enemies within that ultimately lead to self-destruction and the annihilation of the dreams of generations unborn.

A reverent reflection on the sands of time, a look back to look ahead, serves to preserve the past and make room for the future. When this time is looked upon, how will it be described? Will it be used for the betterment of students and the education profession? These are questions that must be pondered. Where will public education be in five years, ten years, and fifteen years?

Just as there is a need to avoid transforming students into mere test-taking soldiers, there must also be an avoidance of turning leaders for learning into bureaucratic nomads, wandering blindly with a singular focus on the next mandate or the next series of compliance measures. The road forward focus-ing on opportunities must be taken to have a positive and lasting impact on students, knowing that the future is merely an infinite series of present mo-ments.

Chapter Eleven

Gates of a New Era

If you've always had privilege, equality feels like oppression.

Education has entered the gates of a new era in which the likelihood and level of success is largely contingent on the level of ambition. Subsequently, there is a call for individuals to lead boldly into unchartered territories. There is a call for individuals and school systems to serve as the beacon of light of hope and hopefulness; a call for those who value the importance, the critical transforming and transcending power of education, to stand up, speak out, and help define the new reform.

While the tone and tenor of the times have been steeped with the exaggeration of negative occurrences in school systems and institutions, education remains as the source of hope in such turbulence. Looking out on the educational landscape reveals optimism, knowing that the legacies of many giants and luminous victories have provided a springboard for paving the way to an even more prosperous future.

Wider fields of opportunity have indeed been fanned open, and the commitment to excellence serves as the turbine that keeps the breeze of opportunity blowing. As such, the provision of high-quality education must be viewed and appreciated as a foundation for futures that are filled with endless possibilities. The dreams of the students, especially the graduates, should be their only limitation on a road of continued success that can be as complicated and paradoxical as its very definition.

Therefore, educators must impart the type of wisdom that engenders feelings of enormous confidence, inspiring students to find their niche, find their calling, and parlay their success into happiness. The ultimate end result is bold pursuits without succumbing to the seductiveness of immediate success and the selfishness of materialism. Through education, destinies are intertwined.

The past collides with the future, and the significance of the present moment is magnified to unprecedented portions, reflecting a marvelous departure from past traditions. As President Barack Obama said, "The arc of history has indeed been bent toward the hope of a better day." The dreams of children are alive in high definition. Today, despite the insecurities of an insecure world, leaders forge ahead with renewed thinking and a renewed sense of importance and priority.

These are the times for students, the next generation of leaders and innovators, of scientist and entrepreneurs, of educators and clergy, of politician and policymakers, parents and advocates, to stand up. It is vital that the voices of students are heard and their presence known, saying enough is enough and putting righteousness in front of greed and sacrifice before self-gratification. The victory of the day is indeed a renewed sense of hope and hopefulness that stokes the fire of motivation, inspiration, and determination to work tirelessly and relentlessly as the trailblazers of justice.

It is a privilege to do the work of fulfilling the promises of learning, facilitating the exploration of new knowledge, and igniting the flame of intellect. A new meaning and an enhanced significance have been placed on the doorsteps of schools. There is too much at risk for us to be shortsighted. Our purpose demands stepping out of the shadows of the past and instructing children to step forward with sturdiness in their walk. This is done with a strident sense of pride to remove the irresolution, contradictions, and hypocrisy.

CATAPULTING MOMENTS

The realization of academic success, like dreams, is an intentional act. There must be an emphatic declaration and a demonstration, going beyond intellectually understanding and articulating an unwavering commitment to excellence. The emphasis is an unwavering commitment, meaning all of the time and with all students, not just those good days or with those favored students. Education as a whole, private and public alike, is challenged with catapulting moments where the very core of educational systems seems to be threatened by severe fiscal constraint coupled with a barrage of reforms.

As such, ambitious and energetic educators need to fortify the commitment to pragmatically embrace the challenges afoot with a keen sense of inventiveness and ingenuity. It is imperative that plans are targeted to effectively fulfill the charge in this era of accountability, an era highlighted by high expectations of proficiency for all. Efforts must be committed to ensuring that the least performing student, colleague, or school is supported and provided the requisite tools for success.

The stakes are high, opinions often vary, and emotions run strong. Hence, there must be a willingness to engage in crucial conversations about what needs to be done, how to best do it, and how progress is effectively measured. The dawn of the "nontraditional" school leader is now. Curriculum and instruction development and academic program planning are still the hallmarks of educational leadership success; however, educational leaders must now be financially, technologically, culturally, and politically savvy.

The proverbial "unfounded mandate" mantras have compelled school leaders to be fiscal leaders and advocates, adequately and consistently completing cost-benefit analysis of programs and services. A thorough understanding of the intricacies of state funding, budgeting, negotiations, human resources (matching task with talents), purchasing, accounting, investing, cash management, and benefit procurement is absolutely critical. Coupled with the aforementioned skills and knowledge is the need to possess comprehensive knowledge of pedagogy, curriculum, and of standards and assessments.

All these skills are vital to "establishing change." Every decision has financial ramifications, and the effectiveness of the implementation is contingent on the fiscal capacity. It is requisite that school leaders of today and tomorrow be competent and prepared to articulate and promulgate the concept of education as an investment rather than an expense. Public schools are functioning in a climate of increasing public scrutiny and calls for accountability. These calls for accountability, however, are not so much about dollars and cents but more so about articulating a vision and effectuating change.

This era of accountability, marked with endless transitions, dictates buckling up and preparing for a ride that is fast and furious. In so many ways students and leaders for learning are embarking upon a world that is filled with the zany and the zealots. Therefore leading must be revolutionary focused and engaged in evolutionary practices. It is the endless pursuit to innovate in a knowledge economy that has redefined the paradigm of past practices and traditions.

In no small token, the future of the world rests with ambitious and aspirational goals. An unwavering willingness to go from success to even greater success is the hallmark trait of effective leadership. Hence, a prerequisite for highly effective leaders is the possession of the zeal to push through the crowd, to press forward, striving to realize the zenith of intellectual capacity. Leaders model the change they want from students and staff alike. Leaders embrace the value of providing a quality education with unabashed appreciation and unwavering passion to seize the moment.

It is truly about living up to the declaration of a commitment to excellence and doing the very best job of helping students achieve their very best. For decades, school systems have made bold declarations of a commitment to excellence. And in many ways they have realized it. Systems must now be able to produce high performance on demand, for every child, every time. The era of accountability calls for moving from bold declarations, to full demonstration, initiation of individual actions, and organizational synergy.

The time has come for leaders for learning to shift the tone and tenor to begin countering the unrelenting punitive tact of recent reforms. Public education cannot be about mandates. Public education cannot be about tests. Public education is about hope and hopefulness. It is about inspiring a sense of inquisitiveness in children.

NO PANACEA: BOLD PURSUITS

It is paramount that educational leaders are capable and prepared to demonstrate bold leadership, which is integral to ensuring that educational pursuits and endeavors are disruptive of the status quo yet structurally sound in design, allowing for seamless execution and replication for institutional growth. There is more than ample room for improvement and enhancement of education systems.

The real quandary is that there isn't a panacea. There is not a silver bullet or even one preeminent method to improve the overall quality of school systems. There are multiple models and many best practices. The leadership focus is on maximizing the shifts that will undoubtedly and inevitably impact not only *what* is taught and assessed, but more significantly, *how* it is taught and assessed to reveal students' progress.

This era demands proficiency in performance by all; subsequently, there must be a firm commitment to lead and work to ensure that children are equipped with the skill sets of being politically sagacious and culturally adept in order to be competitive in the global economy. The result of an education must translate into readiness for the workplace and success in any career. Students must be proficient in:

- Global Literacy—discussing global economic trading partners
- Financial Literacy—understanding the dynamics of the economic marketplace
- Technological Literacy—from digital presentations to virtual online excursions, from the inclusion of mobile devices as a part of the toolkit

Leaders must be confident and committed to assertively guide schools and school systems to the next phase of success.

Clearly the road ahead will not be easy, marked by fiscal uncertainties and prevalent resistance to change and progress while underlined by an increasingly competitive global marketplace. Education leaders must strive to prominently serve as the instrument to effect change and improve the lives of schoolchildren and countless adults.

AGITATE TO EFFECT CHANGE

Schools are microcosms of social ills, and until and unless these harsh realities are faithfully addressed, these malignant effects will persistently manifest. Society is thwarted by the stunning reality that more and more children are being undereducated in increasingly segregated schools. With approximately 30 percent of the nation's public school students attending schools in fifty of the largest cities, and with graduation rates lagging 20 to 35 percent behind counterparts in suburbia, there is an inevitable collision course for disastrous disparities in an increasingly knowledge-driven economy.

There needs to be an agitation of the conversation and messaging to effect change, to stand up and speak truth to power, especially when power is corrupt or misguided. Experience has demonstrated time and time again that the ability to engage in passionate, unfiltered debate about what needs to be done in order for children to succeed will determine the future as much as any program developed or any initiatives implemented. There is a stern difference amid masticating solutions in the jaws of effective dialogue versus the mere spurting of solely contentious barbs to prevent progress.

In the later instance, the penetrating questions about the long-term consequences and implications of poverty and discriminatory practice are not being effectively answered. The perverse irony is that the pain and plight of black and Latino children have become the fuel for the privatization and profiting of public funds for education.

Clearly, there are abysmally performing public schools, and comparably so there are atrociously performing charters. There is no panacea. With that said, there are certain rational agreements:

- Agreement that a quality education stands as the linchpin to empowerment and self-determination
- Agreement that children are capable if their unique needs are recognized, given the opportunity, and held to high expectations
- Agreement that if the accepted belief is that what happens today is a result of what happened yesterday, then it is imperative to change/reform what is done now to preserve a different result tomorrow
- Agreement that educational ineffectiveness not only dwarfs economic potential, it effectively drains the human spirit to pursue dreams and ideals

- Agreement that intergenerational poverty becomes cannibalistic in that it self-perpetuates
- Agreement that strong and courageous leadership leads to positive outcomes

The debate rages upon the articulation, investigation, and dissection of the problem sources:

- Low self-esteem and expectations
- Suspect quality of instruction
- Shallow curriculum and class offerings
- Devaluation of schooling and a lack of culture of learning in communities
- A resegregation of schools, and the staunch impact of inequity and inequality

In the end, the agitation is to effect positive change for all students—black or white, rich or poor, ENLs, disabled or accelerated, the motivated or unmotivated learner. Leaders for learning are the definers of the destiny children need and deserve.

AVANT-GARDE PURSUITS

The issue of failure in school is generational and will require a long-term, steadfast commitment. The same is recognized with the presence of success in schools; it is generational and the expected norm. The problem is deeper than quick-fix reforms. Many students in certain settings, and seemingly more prominent in urban centers, disengage and drop out, not because of innate ability but simply because of environmental models that show the track to college or beyond is not viable or otherwise worth the effort.

Given concrete reasons to succeed, students are more likely to do so. Provided incentives to matriculate in college, students will see it as a possibility. There must be an avant-garde and assiduous pursuit to change: from the perspective of the salvo to the focus of the direction, coming from the flipside of past traditions and practices. It is about truthfully and diligently contending with the harsh realities of institutional racism and discriminatory treatment of certain categories of society. It is about dealing with the documented perpetuation of depressed aspirations of individuals from certain walks of life.

An avant-garde pursuit is about bringing about justice to reverse the genocidal-like effects of the disparate criminalization of children, especially black and Latino males. It is about preemptively preventing failed politics and policies that seem to be more bent on the preservation of the capitalist order. An assiduous pursuit to change the trajectory of system performance entails:

- Providing permissions versus prohibitions
- Creating guidelines to success versus allowances for failure, and
- Cultivating fields of possibilities versus silos of predictability

These pursuits demand a new mantra that speaks to the strengths of public education systems and students, and not the venomous rhetoric that only seems bent on polarization. There needs to be a reinvestment of the public's faith in public education, turning impatience into explicit and positive actions and frustrations into fervent fortitude. Demand excellence and commitment to educate the undereducated and seize hope for the hopeless.

Chapter Twelve

Fuel for the Soul

Excellence without equity is simply privilege, and equity without excellence is merely tokenism.

APHORISMS ABOUT LIFE

1. The past is forgettable—it allows you to move on and precede head-long.
2. The present is forgivable—transgressions and transgressors are not insurmountable or permanent; learn from mistakes.
3. The future is livable—live with an unwavering spirit to give back to others as much as life circumstances provide; dreams are the only limitations.

TEN KEYS TO SUCCESSFUL LEADERSHIP

1. Teams are inherently dysfunctional because they are made up of im-perfect human beings.
2. The man, who insists upon seeing with perfect clarity before he de-cides, never decides.
3. Moments of truth are best handled face to face. In other words, don't send bad news or take on a challenge via e-mail.
4. Honest resistance is necessary to provoke real change.
5. Change is the only constant and stands as the major ingredient for evolutionary progress.
6. The fundamental definition of insanity is doing the same thing over and over again and expecting a different result.
7. Power corrupts, and absolute power corrupts absolutely.

8. True leadership is all about being of a strong mind and a humble heart.
9. Love of mankind is the essence of wisdom.
10. You can be intelligent without being wise, but you can't be wise without being intelligent.

GRATITUDE TO BE AN EDUCATOR

"I am thankful that every day is different. During my day I am given the chance to laugh, smile, and get frustrated, angry, and tearful. I am thankful that being a teacher allows me to see progress in my work. I know that I make a difference because I can see it in the eyes of a child. I am thankful that my job is endless. There will always be children! I am thankful for the long-term progress of my job. I not only can see my work today, but my work continues tomorrow and into the future. I am thankful for the relationships I create. Through the years I have created some very special bonds with children and with families. Few jobs allow the closeness with families that teaching allows. I am thankful for children. I am thankful that I am a teacher." (Mrs. Miller, Seventh-Grade Math Teacher)

"I have never seen the kind of entitlement that exists as it does now, and these are not in the best interests of students. Education is not there to make students feel good, it is a challenge that when attended to, accepted as such, worked with, chewed over and surmounted with a sense of joy and exhilaration, causes a growth that is habit forming and urges the student on to further challenges . . . but not without an initial attitude that the process is worthwhile and necessary." (Mrs. Cutler, Middle School Special Education Teacher)

"QUOTABLES"

- The sacred reward of teaching is being able to make an indelible impression upon the lives of students.
- Enjoy the work and do it well, or have the integrity to leave the occupation.
- It is choice, not chance, that determines destiny, so position for prosperity.
- Never take delay as denial.
- Laughter is fuel for the soul.
- Be forward thinking and optimistic in the face of adversity.
- Challenge opportunities to further manifest an unwavering commitment to excellence.
- Sometimes in the winds of change true direction is found.
- Now is the time to accept the challenge, and now is always.

- Be a positive difference; help students realize their preferred dreams.
- Life is lived forward and understood backward.
- Feel strongly about the work and the privilege to do it.
- Lead with optimism; the future is a bright, luminous place.
- Don't forget that there is more joy in moderation than in excess.
- Life is short, break the rules; forgive quickly; love truly; laugh uncontrollably; and never regret anything that caused a smile.

As Dr. King said, "Through education we seek to change attitudes; through legislation and court orders we seek to regulate behavior. Through education we seek to change internal feelings (prejudice, hate); through legislation and court orders we seek to control the external effects of those feelings. Through education we seek to break down the spiritual barriers to integration; through legislation and court orders we seek to break down the physical barriers to integration. One method is not a substitute for the other, but a meaningful and necessary supplement."

HORSE IN THE RACE

One thing I do to relax is spend some time at the Saratoga Horse Track, watching the horses . . . literally watching the horses. On one occasion I saw a gentleman wearing a $1,000 suit and once very shining shoes now covered with mud, gently sponging down a horse. Being a curious person, there was an urging to know, beyond the obvious, the deeper meaning for the actions. So I asked him. It was simple, yet profound. He said, "This is my horse and when you have a horse in the race you take special care of it . . . you do all the little things to send the message to the horse that you care about its success." He turned and continued gently stroking the side of the horse.

I stood in awe and deep contemplation about what he said. "When you have a horse in the race you take special care . . . you do all the little things to send the message to the horse that you care about its success." Not to sound corny, but I quickly translated that to my job as an educator, as a leader for learning. If he saw it fit to take the extra care with a horse, what am I to do when it comes to kids—the students who rely on us to believe in them, who rely on compassion and caring?

Like that owner and his horse, leading for learning is intrinsically caring about the success of every student, every time. The emphasis there is on the intrinsic versus the extrinsic motivation, being internally passionate and deeply motivated by the simple notion that what is done every day makes a significant and lasting impact on the lives of students, children, sons, and daughters.

Ask questions about the things assumed about the world, and don't be a prisoner of past assumptions. The antidote to solving societal problems and ills is not about sensationalizing and is beyond rationalization. The road of excellence is never ending, often unpaved, uncharted, and traveled with a high degree of trepidation resulting from the constant departure from the comfort of the status quo. This is certainly so in this era of accountability and increased scrutiny of public schools at the federal, state, and local levels. As leaders, we seemingly stand naked in the public eye.